Sierra Nevada
Byways

Sand Canyon Road (Tour 24)

Sierra
Nevada
Byways

50 of the Sierra Nevada's
Best Backcountry Drives

By Tony Huegel

 WILDERNESS PRESS · BERKELEY, CA

Sierra Nevada Byways

1st EDITION 1994
2nd EDITION May 2001
2nd printing May 2002
3rd printing August 2004

Copyright © 2001 by Tony Huegel

All photos, including cover photos, by the author
Maps: Jerry Painter
Cover design: Jaan Hitt
Book design: Jerry Painter

Library of Congress Card Catalog Number 2001017700
ISBN 0-89997-273-X
UPC 7-19609-97273-0

Manufactured in the United States of America

Published by: **Wilderness Press**
1200 5th Street
Berkeley, CA 94710
(800) 443-7227; FAX (510) 558-1696
info@wildernesspress.com
www.wildernesspress.com

Visit our website for a complete listing of our books and ordering information.

Cover photos: *(front)* Laurel Canyon, Sierra Nevada;
(back) Old Stage Stop, White Mountains

SAFETY NOTICE: Although Wilderness Press and the author have made every attempt to ensure that the information in this book is accurate at press time, they are not responsible for any loss, damage, injury, or inconvenience that may occur to anyone while using this book. You are responsible for your own safety and health. The fact that a route is described in this book does not mean that it will be safe for you. Be aware that road conditions can change from day to day. Always check local conditions and know your own limitations.

Library of Congress Cataloging-In-Publication Data
Huegel, Tony.
    Sierra Nevada byways : backcountry drives for the whole family / by Tony Huegel.—2nd ed.
        p. cm.
    Includes indexes.
    ISBN 0-89997-273-X
1. Automobile travel—Sierra Nevada (Calif. and Nev.)—Guidebooks. 2. Sport utility vehicles. 3. Sierra Nevada (Calif. and Nev.)—Guidebooks. 4. Mountain roads—Sierra Nevada (Calif. and Nev.)—Guidebooks. I. Title.
GV1024 .H84 2001
917.94'40454—dc21
                                                            2001017700

Disclaimer

Sierra Nevada Byways has been prepared to help you enjoy backcountry driving. It assumes you will be driving a high-clearance four-wheel drive vehicle that is properly equipped for backcountry travel on unpaved, sometimes unmaintained and primitive backcountry roads. It is not intended to be an exhaustive, all-encompassing authority on backcountry driving, nor is it intended to be your only source of information about the subject.

There are risks and dangers that are inevitable when driving in the backcountry. The condition of all unpaved backcountry roads can deteriorate quickly and substantially at any time. Thus, you may encounter road conditions considerably worse than what is described here. If you drive the routes listed in this book, or any other backcountry roads, you assume all risks, dangers and liability that may result from your actions. The author and publisher of this book disclaim any and all liability for any injury, loss or damage that you, your passengers or your vehicle may incur.

Exercise the caution and good judgment that visiting the backcountry demands. Bring the proper supplies. Be prepared to deal with accidents, injuries, breakdowns and other problems alone, because help will almost always be far away and a long time coming.

Acknowledgments

Many people helped me produce *Sierra Nevada Byways*. First among them are my wife, Lynn MacAusland, and our two children, Hannah and Land. They accompanied me on many of the drives, and put up with prolonged absences while I researched the rest alone.

I couldn't have produced the book without the help of the United States Forest Service and Bureau of Land Management staffers who generously and patiently shared their knowledge. Jerry Painter has yet again made an enormous contribution with the maps he produced for every route in the book. I am indebted as well to Dimitry Struve, who suggested a number of routes that I included in this edition.

Michael Dobrin, of Michael Dobrin Public Relations in Alameda, California, has long provided assistance, support and enthusiasm that helped to make my multistate *Byways* guidebook series possible. I am grateful as well to Toyota Motor Sales, Inc., for providing the comfortable, capable and unfailingly reliable sport-utility vehicles that I use to research the series, which amounts to the ultimate SUV road test. Over thousands of backcountry miles, my family and I have never had a breakdown in a Toyota.

Finally, there is my publisher, Wilderness Press of Berkeley, California. I still have my 1972 edition of *Sierra North*, the backpacking guide that introduced me to the Sierra Nevada. Almost three decades later I'm still getting to know them, and the awe they inspire is undiminished.

Contents

Appendix

Preface

Hiking. Backpacking. Mountain biking. When I was younger, fitter and more footloose, I enjoyed them all. But life always seems to make more, not fewer, demands on our time. Thus, over the years work, family, lawn care and, I must admit, the passing of my physical prime took me away from those once-cherished modes of backcountry travel. As middle age appeared on the horizon, I worried that my days of wandering the wild were over.

Then I discovered that the West's most beautiful and remote regions, occasionally even wilderness areas where mechanized travel is usually prohibited, are crossed by unpaved, often little-known backcountry roads. I learned that with a factory-stock sport-utility vehicle, equipped with high clearance and four-wheel drive, my family and I could have a wild-land experience in the comfort and convenience of our family "car" anytime, whether for a few hours or a few days.

Bringing whatever amenities we wanted, we could explore rugged mountain ranges, high plateaus and remote desert canyons by day and then, if we didn't want to camp, relax at a motel at night. A child in diapers? We could carry a case of them. No time to hike? I could drive. That bothersome foot? It would never hold me back again.

I'd broken free of the limitations of time, distance and physical ability. I'd learned that America's most beautiful wildlands were no longer just for the fit and free, or those who drive motorcycles, ATVs and modified 4x4s. Since many of the West's most rural backroads are relied on by people who live off the land, I found most to be easily driveable, while others were rough enough to provide exhilarating moments of adventure and challenge. I didn't need a winch, a lift kit or oversized tires and wheels.

Over the years, backcountry touring became a bigger and bigger part of my family's outdoor life. With our children, we got to know the beauty and history of the West in ways that would not have been possible for us otherwise.

Sierra Nevada Byways, part of my series of backcountry touring guide-books, will take you along many of the most beautiful and historic unpaved backways in the largest and highest mountain range in the Lower 48. You will experience cool forests, verdant meadows, sky-scraping peaks, glacial basins, high-desert valleys and narrow canyons. You will follow the trails of forty-niners and emigrants over remote mountain passes, through deep river valleys and forgotten ghost towns, on roads that range from primitive 4x4 trails to graded dirt and gravel. Whether you want to get away for a few hours, a day, a weekend or longer, the back-country byways of the Sierra Nevada have just what you're looking for.

Buttermilk Country (Tour 22)

INTRODUCTION

Forestdale Road (Tour 45)

The Sierra Nevada Experience

Roaming The Range of Light

Anyone who has waited in line for a wilderness backpacking permit, a ski lift or a crack at climbing Mt. Whitney knows the appeal of California's Sierra Nevada. And anyone who's joined or just wondered at the dot-com "Gold Rush," cheered a 49'ers touchdown, eaten Central Valley produce watered by Sierra runoff or worn a pair of Levi's has experienced the historic, cultural, economic and environmental influence of the Sierra on the nation's most populous state.

Christened the "Snowy Range" by the Spanish, the Sierra Nevada is the largest and highest single mountain range in the Lower 48, covering almost as much of California as the alps of France, Switzerland and Italy cover of the European landscape. While the Rockies and Appalachians are comprised of a number of individual ranges, the Sierra is one massive, primarily granitic, downward-extending mountain block, what geologists call a batholith. (Thus, the range is correctly referred to in the singular form, Sierra, not Sierras.) The batholith is comprised of individual masses, called plutons.

The Sierra Nevada's blue-ribbon peak, 14,495-foot Mt. Whitney, is the highest in the United States outside of Alaska. Yet Whitney is only about 80 miles from Death Valley's Badwater, which, at 232 feet below sea level, is the lowest point in the western hemisphere. Thirteen Sierra Nevada peaks exceed 14,000 feet. There are other superlatives. Giant sequoias grow more than 300 feet tall. Kings Canyon plunges more than 7,000 feet, deeper than Arizona's Grand Canyon and the Snake River's Hells Canyon. The Owens Valley, a Great Basin trough stretched between the Sierra and the White-Inyo Range, lies 10,000 feet below the highest summits that flank it.

Each year, millions of people take advantage of the easy access to this ultimate outdoor playground. The ski slopes of Mammoth Lakes are about six hours from Los Angeles. It's an easy four hours or so from San Francisco's sprawling suburbs to Yosemite Valley, the beleaguered destination of about four million people a year. Access to the Sierra's wonders is so easy, and the Sierra's recreational offerings are so diverse, that on holiday weekends the nickname Range of Light, coined by conservationist John Muir, could be changed to Range of Headlights.

The Sierra Nevada is some 400 miles long, stretching like a curved spine from the northwest to southwest, from the confluence with the Cascade Range to the Tehachapis north of Los Angeles. For roughly 140 miles of the Sierra's length, between Tioga Road (U.S. 120) through Yosemite National Park in the north to Sherman Pass and Kennedy Meadow roads in the south, no roads cross the Sierra. It is 50 to 80 miles wide, reaching from some of the world's most productive farmlands in the Central Valley to two great deserts, the Great Basin and the Mojave.

Looking at the Sierra today, it's hard to visualize what was here before: a low, rolling plain beneath a primordial sea. The theory of the Sierra's emergence is based on plate tectonics, which accepts that the Earth's crust is a series of moving, colliding and subducting plates. About 250 million years ago the eastbound, oceanic Pacific plate and the westbound, continental North American plate collided. The Pacific plate dove beneath the

North American plate, in a process called subduction, scraping up sediments, stoking volcanic activity and superheating the subterranean rock. Some 200 million years ago a pool of molten rock and magma began to form ten miles below the surface and this would eventually become the Sierra batholith.

About 80 million years ago, as the magma cooled and rose toward (but not to) the surface, uplifting began. Overlying ocean-floor sediments five to ten miles thick were folded, twisted and lifted above sea level, and then eroded. Gold-bearing quartz veins formed as the last of the hot granite cooled. Eventually, the ancestor of the Sierra Nevada began to appear as erosion wore the thick sedimentary cap away. (Remnants of this cap, called roof pendants, can be seen on the crest as darkly colored masses of rock on the uppermost portions of peaks. The vertical "tombstone rocks" one sees in the western foothills are also seabed remnants.) Erosion carried the sediments from atop the Sierra batholith westward, filling today's Central Valley with material 5,000 to 10,000 feet deep. By about 40 million years ago the first draft of the Sierra Nevada consisted of low, rolling granitic hills and broad valleys.

By perhaps 30 million years ago the ancestral Sierra had been eroded to a range a few thousand feet high at most. Then the San Andreas Fault shifted, causing a major uplift. About 25 million years ago a period of volcanism began that buried the northern Sierra and filled the lowland valleys. This period of volcanism ended 5 million years ago, and most of the volcanic material has eroded away.

About 10 to 12 million years ago another period of uplift began. Three million years ago, as the Earth cooled and the first Sierra glaciers formed, it accelerated. The Sierra block was tilted westward. The eastern flank rose higher and more abruptly, leaving the western side with a much more gradual slope. Similar uneven upward pressure lifted the southern segment higher than the northern segment, creating the exceptionally high southern peaks and leaving the lower, northern section sloping downward.

The Sierra Nevada continue to rise, perhaps keeping pace with erosion. The effects of the tectonic collision that gave them birth continue to manifest themselves as well, especially on the eastern side, where the region's obvious and unsettling volcanic and seismic unrest continues.

Today's Sierra would not look as it does without the work of glaciers. From cirques to hanging valleys, long U-shaped canyons and rocky moraines, glaciers left their imprint all over the Sierra.

The Sierra have experienced multiple glacial ice ages. The first was 3 million years ago. The heaviest period of glaciation occurred about 60,000 years ago, when an ice cap 275 miles long and 40 miles wide blanketed the Sierra. The most recent, a mini ice age, was 600 years ago. The glaciers' most famous work was done in Yosemite Valley and its twin, the now inundated Hetch Hetchy Valley. The 60 to 70 tiny glaciers that exist in the Sierra today are from the latter, shorter ice age. The largest of these, Palisades, in the mountains west of Big Pine, covers only one square mile.

HUMAN HISTORY. The Sierra Nevada embodies thousands of years of human history. The stories are told at many locales: the bedrock mortars where Indians once ground acorns, the streamside rock piles where forty-niners panned for gold, the passes crossed by pioneers and railroad-ers, even in the corridor now occupied by Interstate 80, the only interstate across the Sierra.

The discovery of gold in the American River at Sutter's Mill in 1848 spurred one of mankind's greatest and swiftest migrations, an entrepreneurial, multiracial, multiethnic, international rush to get rich in California that has yet to abate. Today, one can hardly imagine American history without that icon of individual initiative, the forty-niner peering hopefully into his pan of fine Sierra gravel.

The saga of the Donner Party was written in the Sierra. Chinese laborers built the most difficult and perilous segment of the transcontinental railroad there. During World War II, thousands of Japanese-Americans were interned at the base of the eastern Sierra, at a pear- and apple-growing center called Manzanar.

What would Los Angeles be today if it hadn't been able to siphon off the waters of the eastern Sierra? Would we eat as well or house ourselves as well without the rivers and forests of the western slope? Imagine the California lifestyle without the legendary ability to drive in a few hours from the ocean to the Gold Country, from the suburbs of San Bernardino to the ski slopes of Mammoth Mountain, or from Lake Tahoe to Death Valley.

The Sierra Nevada forms a dividing line between two worlds. Driving to the Sierra from the populated coastal areas and across the Central Valley, one finds the gently sloping, well-watered western foothills pastoral, quaint and user-friendly. Life is good west of the crest, with upwards of 50 inches of precipitation a year, numerous rivers and lots of roads for those who head for the hills each weekend. Climbing toward the crest, one encounters the Sierra's harder face. The timber grows thick. There is granite everywhere, rock that only glaciers could move. Over Donner, Carson, Monitor or Ebbetts passes, the traveler plunges down one of the steepest mountain escarpments in the world to be greeted by a vast, high desert that lies in the Sierra's rain shadow.

Pacific air currents, moving from west to east, dump their moisture on the Sierra, making them one of the snowiest places anywhere in winter. By the time they reach the eastern side, little moisture is left. So here in the rain shadow, life must make do with five to 15 inches of precipitation a year. Not many people live here, and most who do hug the base of the range, where the snowmelt runs.

Exploitation of the mountains' natural wealth has taken a heavy toll on both the state's native population and ecology. From the use of powerful hydraulic hoses to mine gold, to the cutting of giant sequoias, from overcrowding in Yosemite and development in the Lake Tahoe Basin to the draining of the Owens Valley, humans have inflicted heavy blows.

For those who seek outdoor recreation and adventure surrounded by worldclass beauty, the Sierra arguably exceeds California's two other defining landscapes, the coast and the deserts. For millions of people, the California coast is largely a visual rather than participatory experience. The deserts—where placenames often invoke death and the devil—can inspire trepidation and respect; if we go there at all, we don't stay long. By contrast, the Sierra offers a huge range of year-round activities suited to just about everyone. For a major mountain range, the weather, especially in summer and fall, could hardly be better. From sightseers, campers, climbers, hikers, water skiers, kayakers, anglers and four-wheelers to history buffs, mountain bikers, photographers and snow skiers, anyone can find something fun to do in the Sierra.

To fully appreciate the region dominated by the Sierra one needs to venture not just into the Sierra, but also into the deserts and mountains nearby. Just east of the Sierra stand the White Mountains, the Great Basin's highest. Although they rival the Sierra in height, they could hardly be more different, for they stand in the Sierra's rain shadow. Thus they lack the Sierra's conifer forests, grasslands, lakes and streams. Denied adequate moisture, they never experienced glaciers. Yet the Whites' harsh environment is home to bristlecone pines that are thousands of years old, among the oldest living things on Earth. With roads that climb to well over 11,000 feet, the White Mountains provide a unique high-elevation driving experience through rocky, rolling mountaintops.

South of the Whites, the geologically-linked Inyo Mountains have beautiful canyons, basins and vistas. Even the Sweetwater Mountains, just west of the Nevada line, have soaring peaks, rocky crests and historic mining camps. With regard to the Sierra, these neighboring ranges have something in common besides the rain shadow: all three provide stunning big-picture views of the High Sierra and the vast region it influences.

Throughout the Sierra and its neighboring ranges thread hundreds of miles of unpaved, often little-traveled and little-known backcountry roads. The motoring counterparts to hiking trails, they include some of the most scenic and historic backways anywhere. Many are rudimentary old wagon roads. Some have been used by ranchers for generations. Others are well-maintained, graveled byways. Scratched into mountainsides, over remote passes, through forests, across deserts and subalpine flats, they have been largely overlooked by the general motoring public. Yet they provide fascinating and often exhilarating opportunities to explore the Sierra. They take adventurous travelers up canyons carved by glaciers and across desert expanses paved with ancient lava flows. They follow routes taken by emigrants and forty-niners. They wind past remote Gold Rush camps and ghost towns, through stands of Joshua trees at the desert's edge, to sky-scraping ridges and along plunging river gorges.

The backcountry driving tours in *Sierra Nevada Byways* will take you far from the crowds, off the beaten path and beyond the standard tourist route. All you have to do is turn the page, then turn the key.

Adventuring in Your SUV

Backcountry Touring 101

Sierra Nevada Byways is intended to introduce backcountry touring to people who travel in factory-stock, high-clearance four-wheel drive sport-utility vehicles equipped for possibly rough off-highway conditions. Since relatively few people who drive SUVs take advantage of what their vehicles can do, I'm going to assume that your experience is limited, and provide some basic know-how. My hope is to help you have a safe and enjoyable experience while protecting the Sierra's natural environment as well as its historic and cultural sites.

KNOW YOUR VEHICLE. Some automakers, eager to tap into the motoring public's yen for at least the visage of adventure, have begun to apply the label "sport-utility" to just about anything with wheels. Don't be fooled. Know what you're driving, and drive within the vehicle's limits as well as your own.

Familiarize yourself with your SUV's four-wheel drive system. Is it a full-time, part-time or automatic system? In a full-time, or permanent, 4WD system, all four wheels are continuously engaged as driving wheels; there is no 2WD mode. (A multi-mode system, however, will include a 2WD mode.) Full-time 4WD uses either a center differential or viscous coupling to allow the front and rear axles to turn independently for typical daily driving. Some systems allow the driver to "lock" the center differential so that, in poor conditions, both axles will turn together for greater traction. A part-time system uses only the rear wheels as driving wheels until the driver engages 4WD. A part-time system must be disengaged from 4WD on pavement to avoid excessive drivetrain stress. An automatic system is designed to sense on its own when 4WD should be engaged. All-wheel-drive (AWD) systems, such as those used in some passenger cars and vans, provide power to all four wheels much as full-time 4WD systems do. But AWD vehicles are usually designed for all-weather use, not all-terrain use.

Does your vehicle have a transfer case? More than any other single feature, a transfer case identifies a vehicle suited to all-terrain travel. It sends power to the front axles as well as to the rear axles, and, acting as an auxiliary transmission, provides a wider range of gear ratios for a wider range of driving conditions. Use high-range 2WD for everyday driving in normal conditions, both on pavement and off. Use high-range 4WD when added traction is helpful or necessary on loose or slick surfaces, but when conditions are not difficult. Use low-range 4WD in difficult low-speed conditions when maximum traction and power are needed, and to keep engine revs high while moving slowly through rough or steep terrain.

Does the vehicle have all-season highway tires or all-terrain tires? Tires take a terrible beating in off-highway conditions, for which the latter are designed.

Find out where the engine's air intake is, and how high it is. This is important to avoid the devastating consequences of sucking water into the engine through the air intake while fording waterways.

Does the vehicle have steel "skid plates" protecting undercarriage components like the engine oil pan, transfer case and transmission? Skid plates are essential to avoiding the expensive and very inconvenient damage that obstacles, particularly roadbed rocks, can inflict.

KNOW WHERE YOU'RE GOING. The maps in this book are general locator maps only. For route-finding you will need a good statewide map in addition to a detailed map illustrating the area you will be visiting and the route you'll be driving.

Each tour description in *Sierra Nevada Byways* recommends at least one map for route-finding. These maps often will include other useful information about the area's natural and human history, regulations, campgrounds, picnic areas and historic sites. They often differentiate between public and private lands as well. The Forest Service's national forest visitor maps may be the best all-purpose maps, but some are out of date and may depict road numbers that no longer apply, campgrounds that have become picnic areas, and roads that are now closed or whose quality has changed. Occasionally, the number on a roadside signpost will not match what is shown on the map. In some cases, different national forest maps will depict the quality of the same road differently. So buy the latest map available. Maps of various kinds can be purchased at Forest Service and United States Bureau of Land Management offices, bookstores, information centers and outdoor recreation equipment stores, as well as from Wilderness Press, (800) 443-7227.

Go over your maps before you begin the drive. Become familiar with sights and landmarks to watch for along the way, and as you travel keep track of your progress to avoid missing important turnoffs, places of interest and side trips.

Don't expect to find road signs. The agencies that manage backcountry roads and the wildlands they cross do post signs, but they don't last long. Vandals, especially the gun-toting kind, make short work of them. If you reach a junction where there are several routes to choose from and none has a sign, it's usually best to follow what appears to be the most heavily used route.

Global Positioning System navigation units are increasingly popular. I'm sure some backroad travelers find them handy at times, especially when they're trying to pinpoint a hard-to-find point of interest. However, I have not yet found a GPS unit to be necessary.

When venturing into unfamiliar territory, it's sometimes best to rely on road numbers rather than road names because rural and backcountry roads sometimes have more than one name. You will quickly find that roads can have more than one numerical designation as well. Counties, for example, may assign a number that is different from the one used by the U.S. Forest Service.

As you wander the wild, remember that the settlers, ranchers, miners and loggers who made these roads didn't have your safety in mind.

WEATHER AND WHEN TO GO. The Sierra is the largest and highest mountain range in the Lower 48, and the greater Sierra region has a wide range of climatic zones. The Sierra Nevada does its part to perpetuate California's "sunshine state" image, providing visitors with exceptionally good mountain weather in summer and fall. While visitors to the Colorado Rockies can count on violent summertime thunderstorms, and even snow by mid-September, travelers in the Sierra can reasonably expect sunny days and tentless nights. *Sierra Nevada Byways* will take you over 11,000 feet in elevation, from the foothills and the high desert to subalpine basins. The deserts at the foot of the eastern escarpment are hot and dry in summer. The lower foothills also are dry in summer (and fire-prone), and can get darn hot as well. Above, say, 4,500 feet things cool off considerably, especially once you enter the fir and pine forests.

In spring, streams can be swollen with runoff, but the desert lands east of the Sierra can be a colorful palette of wildflowers. Lower forest roads can be muddy through June or early July. A road that is clear for miles can remain blocked as late as August by a slow-melting, late-season snowdrift lingering in a single spot of shade.

Pay attention to the sky, even the sky off in the distance, in case a storm is brewing. Stay out of washes and narrow canyons if a storm seems likely. When it rains, many dirt roads can become dangerously slick. Some may become impassable, even with 4WD. Danger aside, driving on muddy roads leaves tracks that can erode into major ruts, so avoid doing so.

I particularly enjoy September and early October. Daytime temperatures are mild, the aspens are turning color and the sunlight is taking on its golden autumn hue. Remember that the days are growing shorter by then, and you may want to avoid driving these roads at night.

The consistently fine Sierra Nevada weather can lull you into potentially dangerous complacency. Generally, plan on going from late spring through fall at the lower elevations, and mid-summer to early fall higher up.

Finding out the latest road conditions can be difficult. Visitor centers and small, outlying ranger stations are often staffed by volunteers who can help with campground locations and such, but may not know the back-country roads very well. The most knowledgeable people at the Forest Service and Bureau of Land Management, which oversee vast expanses of public lands, are often out in the field. Their ability to monitor conditions along remote backcountry roads and trails is limited. You will often just have to go see for yourself.

GOING ALONE. There is security in having more than one vehicle, and more than one source of ideas and labor if things go awry in rough terrain. It's also fun to be with other people, but when you're on vacation, you and yours will probably go alone, in a single vehicle. That's OK as long as you have a reliable vehicle and are prepared to handle emergencies on your own.

You won't always have the road to yourself. To the contrary, Californians love their backroads. Tourists do, too. Exploring backcountry roads is becoming an increasingly popular form of recreational driving. While the more remote roads may provide genuine solitude, you will be sharing other routes with all sorts of users, from mountain bikers and hikers to all-terrain vehicle riders, ranchers and loggers. Be alert, and be considerate.

RULES OF THE ROAD. Even in places where no one will be watching, there are rules to follow, and practices that help to preserve natural and historic areas. The intent behind them is simple: to keep you safe, to keep your vehicle operating reliably, and to protect fragile wildlands and cultural sites from abusive and destructive activities. Misconduct and mistakes can result in personal injury, damage to your vehicle, areas being closed and perhaps even legal penalties.

Here are some things to keep in mind:
- Drive only on established roads where motor vehicles are permitted. Mechanized travel of any kind, including motorcycles and mountain bikes, is not allowed in designated wilderness areas and wilderness study areas unless a legal corridor exists. Never go "off-road," make a new route, or follow the tracks of someone who did.
- Do not disturb archaeological or historic sites or artifacts. They are not replaceable, and are protected from theft and vandalism by federal laws. Do not touch Native American rock art. Treat historic structures like the important relics of bygone times that they are.
- Do not use archaeological or historic sites for picnics or camping unless they are developed for those purposes. The more time people spend at them, the more they are degraded.
- Your vehicle must be street legal to take these drives. Obey traffic laws and regulatory signs, wear your seat belt, and keep the kids buckled up.
- If you get lost or stuck, stay with your vehicle unless you are certain help is nearby. A vehicle will be much easier for searchers to find than you will be if you're out there wandering aimlessly.
- Some of the places you will visit remain honeycombed with old mines that pose many dangers. View them from a distance.
- Dangerous blind curves are common. Round them carefully.
- If you camp, use minimum-impact practices and leave no trace of your stay. Camp only at established campsites or areas that show previous use. Bring your own water (many developed campgrounds are dry now due to changing water-quality standards), and camp at least 300 feet from the banks of streams, ponds and lakes to avoid damage and pollution, and to allow access by wildlife. Clean up the campsite before you leave, and take your trash and wastes with you.
- Never camp in desert washes or narrow canyons, especially in summer when the desert's inability to absorb sudden downpours creates flash floods that can instantly sweep you and your vehicle away.
- Leave gates as you find them. Don't disturb livestock.
- Don't drink directly from streams, which can be contaminated by that longtime bane of backpackers, the parasite *giardia*.
- Avoid parking on grass, because hot exhaust systems can ignite fires.
- Avoid steep hillsides, stream banks and boggy areas.

GO PREPARED. Things can and will go wrong out there, so be prepared to handle problems alone, perhaps even to spend a night or two. Here's a basic checklist of some things to bring:
- A topped-off fuel tank. Fill up before every backcountry drive, every time. You will use your vehicle's low gears much of the time, which will mean higher fuel consumption than during on-highway driving. It shouldn't be necessary to carry extra fuel. If you do, strap the container to the exterior of the vehicle, preferably the roof. Keep the container full so that dangerous fumes won't build up inside.
- A shovel. Mine has been a life-saver, and is the single most useful tool I carry. Yours will be, too.
- A good first-aid kit, food and drinks, and clothing for inclement weather.
- Good all-terrain tires, a good (and properly inflated) spare and jack, a small board to support the jack on dirt, a couple of cans of pressurized tire sealant (available at department stores), a small electric air

compressor (the kind that plugs into the cigarette lighter, also available at department stores), a tire pressure gauge and tire chains. *A warning: Old mine sites and ghost towns are often littered with old, rusty nails.*

- Some basic tools, including a folding saw (for removing deadfall), jumper cables, duct tape, electrical tape, baling wire, spare fuses, multipurpose knife, high-strength tow strap, fire extinguisher, and a plastic sheet to put on the ground. An assortment of screws, washers, nuts and such could come in handy as well, especially if you're driving an older or modified (meaning trouble-prone) vehicle.
- Maps, compass, extra eyeglasses and keys, binoculars, trash bags, flashlight or head lamp with extra batteries, matches, watch, hats, sunscreen, insect repellent.

Except for the food, I keep much of this stuff ready to go in a large plastic storage container. It's also important to tie it all down so it doesn't get tossed about when you're in the rough.

Sometimes I bring my mountain bike as a backup vehicle. Since I do a lot of exploring, I also use it to check out places that I don't want to drive to. Consider getting a CB radio and roof antenna, even though transmitting range is limited. These days, a cellular telephone can be handy, although I've found they often don't work in the wild.

OFF-HIGHWAY DRIVING. Driving more slowly and cautiously than you do on paved roads will get you where you want to go and back again most of the time. Here are some tips for those inevitable times when the going will get rough:

Uphill traffic has the right of way. If practical, it is usually easier and safer to back up to a pullout, using gravity as a brake, than to back down a slope while fighting the pull of gravity.

Think ahead. If you have a part-time 4WD system, engage it before you need it to stay out of trouble.

When in doubt, scout. If the road ahead seems dicey, walk it and see.

Air down in sand, deep mud and rocky terrain. While standard tire pressure usually will suffice, deep mud and soft, dry sand may require temporarily airing down (letting air out) to 15-18 psi or even lower to expand the tire's "footprint" for greater flotation. Dampening dry sand with water can firm it up. On rocky terrain, airing down will soften the ride and lessen the punishment the roadbed inflicts on the suspension. On especially rocky and steep terrain, airing down also will allow the tires to conform to the rocks so they can grip better. Shallow mud can be underlain by firm ground, so normal tire inflation or even over-inflation can help tires penetrate to terra firma.

Remember to re-inflate the tires before driving at speed or on pavement, using a small electric air compressor if necessary.

Maintain steady forward momentum in sand, mud and snow. Often, stopping can be the worst thing to do, so go as slow as you can, but as fast as you must. Higher gears can be more effective than lower gears.

Because of the range of problems that driving in mud poses (roadbed damage, vehicle damage, transporting biological organisms from one ecosystem to another), avoid it. If it rains, pull onto firm ground and let the storm pass. Then wait an hour or so to let the road dry out.

If you begin to lose traction in mud, turn the steering wheel rapidly one way and then the other, back and forth. That can help the tires get a grip.

If you do get stuck, dig out the sides of the tires to relieve suction. Then pack debris around the tires for traction.

Dust storms and flash floods are dangerous. Blinding dust storms can kick up suddenly in the desert. Do not attempt to drive through one. Instead, pull over to a safe place, turn off the engine to avoid clogging the air filter, and wait it out, keeping windows and doors closed.

In spring, and during and after summer storms, you are likely to encounter flooded roads. Check the depth and speed of the water before fording. If it's fast and deep, stay out and come back in a few weeks if you can.

Stick to the high points. When the going gets particularly rough, shift into low range, go slow and steady, and keep the tires on the high spots, thus keeping the undercarriage high and away from obstacles that can damage the differentials, or so-called "pumpkins," or other components. Let the tires roll over the rocks. Do not let large rocks pass directly beneath the vehicle.

All thumbs? You won't be for long if you forget to keep them on top of the steering wheel. Otherwise, the wheel's spokes can badly injure your thumbs if a front wheel is suddenly jerked in an unexpected direction. If the steering wheel is being rocked back and forth by the terrain, keep your hands loose on the wheel, at 10 and 2 o'clock.

Another tip for rough conditions: Lean forward, keeping your back away from the seat back, and ride as though you're in a saddle. That way you won't be tossed about so much.

Straddle ruts. Let them pass beneath the vehicle. If you must cross a rut, do so at an angle, easing one tire at a time across it. Do the same for depressions, dips, ledges or "steps," and ditches.

If you get stuck: raise the vehicle with a good jack (not the bumper-mounted kind) and fill in the space beneath and around the affected wheels with dirt and debris until you've created a ramp (it can help to make it high enough so that the wheel's on a downslope).

To get over a ledge: either use the rock ramp that is likely to be there already, or use a few nearby rocks to build one. You may need to put one wheel over at a time.

A word about earth-moving: If you've had to build a rudimentary ramp to get over an obstacle or out of a rut, afterwards put the dirt and rocks back where you found them. Don't leave an excavation site behind.

Be prepared to remove deadfall from the roadway. Occasionally you may encounter a fallen tree or limb in the road. It's usually possible to drive around it. If you must drive over it, approach at an angle and put one wheel at a time over it. If you carry a folding saw, as I do, cut it away. If the obstacle is too large to cut or move by hand, consider using your tow strap to pull it out of the way.

Have someone act as a spotter. This will help you maneuver through difficult places. Use low range and a low gear for better control.

Try not to spin your tires. This tears up the road and can get you stuck, or stuck worse than you already may be. Some new SUVs have sophisticated 4-wheel electronic traction-control systems that are intended to eliminate wheel spin by instantly transferring power from spinning wheels to the wheel or wheels with traction. A few, like Toyota's 4Runner and Land Cruiser, can be purchased with locking differentials, a.k.a. "lockers." These mechanisms vastly improve your ability to get through or out of nasty off-highway situations by equalizing power to the driving wheels and eliminating the differential's tendency to transfer power to the wheel with the least traction. I recommend them.

Some hills will be badly chewed up by the spinning tires of vehicles that lack locking differentials or traction control systems. If you encounter such a hill, shift into low range and keep your wheels on the high spots between the holes.

If your vehicle gets high-centered, that is, the undercarriage is hung up atop an obstacle like a rock, jack it up and see if the obstacle can be removed. Or build small ramps, using dirt and rocks, beneath the tires so you can drive off the obstacle.

Before climbing over a steep, blind hilltop, learn what's up there and on the other side. Depending on how steep it is and how much power your vehicle has, shift into first or second gear/low range. Drive straight up, accelerate as you climb, keep moving, then slow down as you near the top.

If the engine stalls on a hill, stop and immediately set the parking brake hard and tight. Here, an automatic transmission can help you get going again easily. Just shift into "park" and turn the key. If you have a manual transmission, you may be able to compression-start the engine if you're facing downhill. If you're facing uphill, try shifting into first gear/low range. Turn the engine over without clutching, and let the starter motor move things along a bit until the engine starts and takes over. Otherwise, you'll have to work the clutch, hand brake and accelerator simultaneously to get going again without rolling backward. Modern clutch-equipped vehicles require the driver to depress the clutch pedal to start the engine, which is fine in a parking lot but difficult on a steep mountain incline. However, some SUVs have clutch bypass switches that let you start the engine without depressing the clutch, a great help when stalled on a climb.

If you can't make it up a hill, don't try to turn around. Stop, and put the transmission in reverse/low range. Tilt the exterior mirrors, if you can, so that you can see what the rear tires are doing. Then slowly back straight down. Never descend in neutral, relying on the brakes. If you must apply the brakes, do so lightly and steadily to avoid losing traction and going into a slide. Go straight down steep inclines, using low range and the lowest driving gear so the engine can help brake. But remember that automatic transmissions, which I think are best overall, don't provide as much engine-braking ability as manual transmissions.

Avoid traversing the side of a steep hill. Occasionally, though, mountain roads do cross steep slopes, sometimes tilting the vehicle "off-camber," or toward the downhill side. It's almost always an unnerving experience for me, especially if the road has become wet and perhaps a bit slick. Lean heavily (no pun intended) toward caution under such circumstances. You might want to remove cargo from the roof to lower your vehicle's already-high center of gravity. Then go slow. It might help to turn the front wheels into the hill. If you decide not to continue, do not attempt to turn around. Tilt the exterior mirrors so you can watch the rear tires, shift into reverse/low range for greater low-speed control, and slowly back up until you reach a spot where you can turn around safely.

Avoid crossing waterways if you can. Fording streams and shallow rivers is fun, to be sure. But many living things reside in or otherwise depend on streams, and can be harmed by careless and unnecessary crossings that stir up sediment and erode stream banks. If you must cross, use an established crossing point. Check with a stick if you're unsure of its

Cross Sierra streams slowly and carefully

depth, comparing the depth to your vehicle. Or walk across first. Don't cross if the current is fast and deep. Never enter a desert wash if it's flooding. Check for deep holes. Often, a somewhat fast-moving perennial stream will be safer to cross than a sluggish one, because continuously moving water prevents sediments from settling, keeping the bed rocky and firm. Slow-moving or still water, on the other hand, lets sediment and mud build up.

A slow, steady crossing will stir up less sediment, and will make less of a bow wake, thus minimizing stream bank erosion and the impact on plants and wildlife. (In particularly deep water, however, a bow wake can create a beneficial air pocket for the engine.)

Be aware of where your engine's air intake is. It may not be high enough to ford deep water. If it isn't, it could suck water into the engine, causing severe damage.

In deep crossings, it's also possible for water to be drawn into your vehicle's gear boxes unless the differential vents have been raised to a point that will keep them above the water. (To avoid that, I've extended my 4Runner's front and rear differential vents up into the engine compartment, using long sections of hose. This also helps to keep them clear of dust and dirt, which can clog them, causing interior pressure to build up and seals to leak.) I try to avoid water that is higher than the wheel hubs.

Once across, stop and inspect the vehicle. The brakes will be wet, so use them a few times to dry them out. The tires also will be wet, and may not grip the roadbed as well.

SUVS, ACCESSORIES AND SUCH. Properly equipped sport-utility vehicles are built to take people to places that sedans, vans and station wagons either cannot go, or shouldn't. Despite their comforts, they are rugged and reliable transport—backcountry or frontcountry. They can go from the showroom straight into the hills without modifications.

One of my family's two Toyota 4Runners has a 5-speed manual transmission and a stock 4-cylinder engine, which I've found to be adequate even when it's loaded with the four of us and our camping gear. The other has a relatively fuel-frugal V6 and automatic transmission. I've never felt any need for a large, thirsty V8.

Manual transmissions have advantages. They are more responsive and tend to provide slightly better fuel mileage and are better at engine braking on steep terrain. Many clutch-equipped vehicles require the driver to fully depress the clutch pedal when starting the engine, which can be a problem if you're stalled on a steep hill. However, on a steep incline you can put the transmission in first gear/low range and let the starter motor start the engine while it simultaneously pulls the vehicle forward. It's also possible to compression-start the engine if the starter or battery dies.

I prefer automatic transmissions. I find them easier to use when the going is rough, where having a manual transmission can require three feet: one for the brake, one for the clutch and one for the accelerator, all working pretty much simultaneously.

I've learned to appreciate options that I once dismissed as unnecessary. Easily adjusted electric side mirrors, for example, will pay for themselves the first time you have to back up a narrow shelf road with a killer drop-off. When I'm exploring narrow, high-walled canyons, a sunroof/moonroof is a handy option indeed.

There is a huge four-wheel-drive accessories market. Are those add-ons necessary? It depends on how much, and what type of adventure motoring you plan to do. The requirements of serious four-wheeling on technically challenging routes differ from those of backcountry touring. The former can require extensive vehicle modifications, which can degrade on-highway performance and reliability. The latter does not. Still, if you enjoy traveling the West's vast network of backcountry roads, there can be real benefits to adding extra lights, beefier tires, a more versatile roof carrier, heavier skid plates, perhaps even an after-market locking differential to your SUV. (In case you're wondering, I've never owned a winch.)

Maintenance is essential. Backcountry roads are hard on all vehicles, so follow the recommendations in your owner's manual for dusty, wet and muddy conditions.

Check the tires often, because no part of your SUV will take a greater beating. If you pass through an old mining area, expect to pick up a nail now and then. Always travel with a good spare, properly inflated.

Wash your vehicle when you return to town to prevent rust and corrosion. You also don't want to carry home the mud, dirt and debris that has collected underneath, because transporting spores, insects and other organisms to disparate geographic regions via off-highway vehicles can spread pests and diseases.

HAVE FUN. Backcountry roads provide terrific opportunities to explore the Sierra Nevada easily and conveniently. If you're particularly interested in preserving the privilege, you might join Tread Lightly!, Inc., a non-profit organization based in Ogden, Utah, founded to promote responsible use of off-highway vehicles. Call 1-800-966-9900.

And as you travel, tell me what you've found, whether they are mistakes or trips and tips you'd like to see added to future editions. You can write to me in care of Wilderness Press, 1200 Fifth St., Berkeley, CA 94710, email: *mail@wildernesspress.com*.

Making It Fun For All

Trying to keep kids happy on car trips is tough. But there are things you can do to make touring the backcountry fun for them.

- Don't just drive. Stop, and stop often. Watch for wildlife, especially early in the morning or evening. Visit the historic sites that *Sierra Nevada Byways* will guide you to. Let the kids see a bit of what life was like in the old mining camps, ghost towns and settlements that echo California history.

- Pick up a book or two that will help you identify, understand and explain the Sierra's history, scenery, diverse vegetation and life zones, and wildlife. I enjoy looking up the story behind place names. You will find all sorts of references, for adults as well as children, at local visitor centers throughout the Sierra.

- Make a photocopy of the area on the map where you'll be going. Let the kids help you navigate and identify peaks, creeks, historic sites and other landmarks.

- Bring at least one personal cassette or CD player (the latter will need good anti-shock protection so that playback is not affected by road bumps). If you have small children, check out some children's cassette tapes or CDs from your public library. They've been lifesavers for my family on many long trips. Audio books, which I listen to myself on long drives, are great diversions for children as well. Many video rental stores carry them.

- Other items that have helped to sustain the kids' interest are an inexpensive point-and-shoot camera they can use, and inexpensive binoculars.

- If you have a licensed teenage driver on board, let him or her drive now and then. The sooner a teen learns backcountry driving skills, the longer he or she will remain an eager participant. And someday you may need a capable co-pilot.

- Bring snacks, preferably the non-sticky kind, and drinks. There will be plenty of bumps on your adventures, so cups with spill-proof tops are essential. Plastic garbage bags, paper towels, changes of clothing, wet wipes and pillows are good to have along, too.

Whether you travel with children or not, make the drive part of a day that draws on the huge range of experience the Sierra Nevada has to offer. Plan a picnic. Hike to a hilltop. Ride your mountain bikes. And do something civilized when you get back to town: Go out to dinner.

How to Use
Sierra Nevada Byways

LOCATION: Where the drive is.

HIGHLIGHTS: What's best about the drive.

DIFFICULTY: This is subjective, since opinions and levels of experience will differ. Conditions can and do change, as well. I assume you are not a serious four-wheeler, but somebody traveling in a stock, high-clearance 4-wheel-drive (4WD) vehicle with all-terrain tires and a transfer case with high and low range. That said, the ratings are: *easy*, which means it's a cruise that probably won't require using 4WD unless conditions deteriorate; *moderate*, which means slower going using 4WD much of the time, with rough spots, possible stream fordings, deep ruts, etc., but little or no technical terrain; and *difficult*, which means at least some technical four-wheeling, rough and slow going in 4WD/low range, and the possibility that you will scrape the undercarriage or even the body panels.

TIME & DISTANCE: The approximate time it takes to complete the drive, excluding travel time getting to the starting point and any stops you might make along the way. Since odometer accuracy varies among vehicles, your measurements of distances may differ somewhat from mine.

MAPS: Each tour description is accompanied by a locator map, with the route highlighted. These maps should not be used for route-finding. For that, I list maps that provide greater detail. Choose one, and refer to it along the way. Since most of the drives are located in or near national forests, I usually recommend the U.S. Forest Service (USFS) visitor map produced for the national forest where the route is located. I also cite maps produced by AAA affiliates Automobile Club of Southern California (ACSC) and the California State Automobile Association (CSAA). Occasionally, I will recommend U.S. Geological Survey (USGS) maps as well. Sometimes I cite a supplementary brochure that can be useful. You can usually obtain the maps and brochures from the information sources listed, or from outdoor recreation supply stores, book and map retailers, AAA travel stores and Forest Service offices. Other maps are available through Wilderness Press at (800) 443-7227 or www.wilderness-press.com.

INFORMATION: An agency that may provide current road conditions and other information. Telephone numbers, addresses and Internet Web sites (current at the time of publication) are listed at the back of the book.

GETTING THERE: How to reach the starting point. I typically describe routes going in a particular direction to help you locate and identify landmarks more easily. Many drives can be taken in the opposite direction.

REST STOPS: Places to picnic, camp, or see a historic or cultural site, etc.

THE DRIVE: In this section I provide details of the drive, such as historical background and historic sites, what turns to take, how far it is from point to point and what you will see along the way. I provide odometer readings to help you stay on track.

Map Symbols

Point of interest	■	Information		?
Paved road	▬▬	Hiking trail		- - ⌒ - - -
Easy dirt road	≈≈≈	Forest or county road		3S01
Primitive road	≈ ≈ = = ⌣	Interstate highway		5
Camping	⛺	U.S. highway		101
Lake	🪣	State highway		1
Waterway	～⌒～	North indicator		↑ N
Mountain	⌒⌒			
Ranger station	⬆	**Tours in shaded background**		
Picnic area	🏕	Paved road	～～	
City or town	○	Easy dirt road	～～	
		Primitive road	～～	

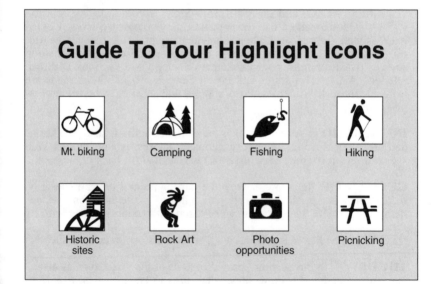

Guide To Tour Highlight Icons

Mt. biking   Camping   Fishing   Hiking

Historic sites   Rock Art   Photo opportunities   Picnicking

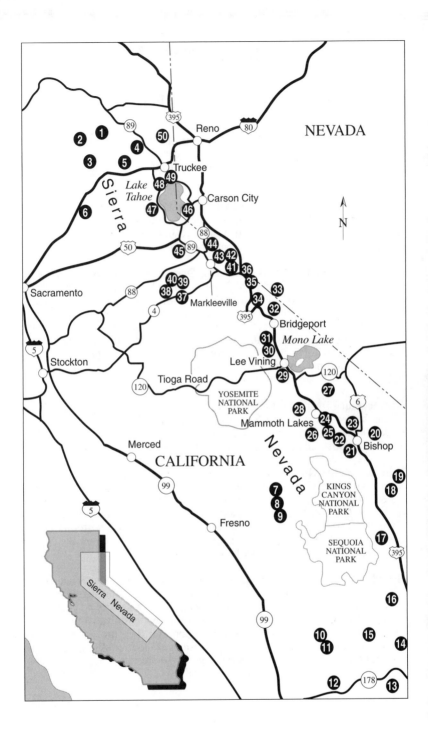

Author's Favorites

Diggins I (Tour 2) & Diggins II (Tour 3): Forty-niners and later 19th century Argonauts who sifted the gravels of the Sierra's streams, washed away entire mountainsides and bored into the rock searching for gold left a legacy that is still visible in the region of the northern mines. These tours take you to the rugged mountains and remote canyons, gullies and streams where not only gravel was washed away in the search for riches, but many golden dreams as well.

Jawbone-Lake Isabella (Tour 13): This southern Sierra tour is fascinating not only for the terrific scenery, but also because it crosses multiple life zones, from the pale canyons and washes of the Mojave Desert to Joshua tree woodlands, stands of oak and high conifer forest.

The Narrows-Papoose Flat (Tour 19): One way to get an overall view of the Sierra Nevada is to drive high into a neighboring range from which you can view the Sierra. This drive into the Inyo Mountains, which stand east of the Sierra, provides superlative views of the Sierra and lets you experience the drying effect of the Sierra's rain shadow. It won't take more than a few minutes to discover that, from their deep canyons to their rocky flats and lofty peaks, the Inyo Mountains are a spectacular and equally rewarding destination by themselves. If you're looking for solitude as well as beauty and adventure, the Inyos are hard to beat.

Coyote Flat (Tour 21): From the high-desert Owens Valley to subalpine basins below some of the Sierra's highest and most spectacular alpine peaks, this tour has it all. The scenery ranks among the best the Sierra has to offer. It's just outside of Bishop, the bustling hub of the Owens Valley.

Wheeler Ridge Road (Tour 25): This exhilarating drive in the eastern Sierra will satisfy those seeking a high-elevation four-wheeling experience amid the Sierra's famous granite. With care, it's do-able in a stock SUV equipped with a transfer case and skid plates (I drove it in a new Toyota 4Runner without any trouble). It will reward you with one of the most breathtaking vistas of the Sierra, the Owens Valley and the White Mountains that you'll find anywhere.

Boulder Flat (Tour 33) & Jackass Flat (Tour 35): The Sweetwater Mountains, like the Inyos and the Whites, rise east of the Sierra. As with those other ranges, they are in many ways (publicity and crowds included) eclipsed by the Sierra. The Sweetwaters also provide outstanding views of the alpine spine of their dominant neighbor. But they are an impressive mountain range in their own right, with magnificent peaks, high ridges, colorful basins, historic sites, everything but the crowds.

THE DRIVES

Sierra Buttes from Upper Sardine Lake (Tour 1)

Sierra Buttes Lookout (Tour 1)

Sierra Buttes Loop

LOCATION: North of Hwy. 49 at Sierra City. Tahoe National Forest.

HIGHLIGHTS: This 4WD adventure includes a shelf road and awesome views of the historic North Yuba River Valley and northern Sierra. The tour is capped with 360-degree views from the lookout atop 8,587-foot Sierra Buttes, rock spewed from an undersea volcano 350 million years ago.

DIFFICULTY: Easy to moderate. The first 4.7 miles are a narrow shelf road. To reach the buttes, drive up a steep, moderately difficult 4WD road to a parking area. From there you must hike uphill for a mile or so, then climb 176 stairs to the lookout.

TIME & DISTANCE: With the hike to the lookout, it's about 4.5 hours and 16.5 miles for the entire loop from Sierra City to Sierra Buttes, then down to Bassetts, on Hwy. 49. (It's about 2 hours and 6.8 miles from Sierra City to the parking area below the lookout.) Allow about 50 minutes for the uphill hike to the lookout, on a rocky 4WD road that is closed to motor vehicles.

MAPS: USFS' *Lakes Basin, Sierra Buttes and Plumas-Eureka State Park*. USGS' *Sierra City* topographic map.

INFORMATION: Tahoe NF, Downieville Ranger District.

GETTING THERE: In Sierra City (on Hwy. 49), turn north onto Butte Street. Follow it a short distance to a Y, at Sierra Buttes Road. Go left, and follow the signs for Buttes Lookout and the garbage disposal site. About a mile from town is a gate. The pavement ends here. The route, forest road 93-2 (Sierra County road S520), makes a hard right.

REST STOPS: Sierra City and Bassetts have food and fuel, and there are campgrounds in the area. Visit the nearby Kentucky Mine Museum, east of Sierra City.

THE DRIVE: From pavement's end, continue climbing above the valley of the North Yuba River. The mountainside road is rocky and loose, and in some places the brush extends into the roadway. Now and then you will get glimpses of craggy Sierra Buttes. At mile 3.6, pull over to the left and walk out to a knoll overlooking the valley. An even better view is at mile 4.7 where a small road branches to the left (west), ending in 0.2 mile at Blue Point, where there is a terrific vista across Sierra valleys, canyons and foothills. 0.1 mile from the Blue Point spur, just around the bend to the right (east), a small, signed but unnumbered road branches into the trees at right. (This road isn't shown on the USFS maps.) Take it. In 0.4 mile it will bring you to the Sierra Buttes 4WD road (9323), again on the right. (After visiting the buttes, you will take the road ahead down past Packer Lake to Bassetts.) Shift into low range, and climb 1.1 miles to the parking area. Hike up to the lookout for one of the Sierra's most impressive vistas. (Near the top you'll see names and dates from the late 1800s carved into a large rock.) Backtrack down the 4WD trail, and drive down to Bassetts on graveled and paved roads.

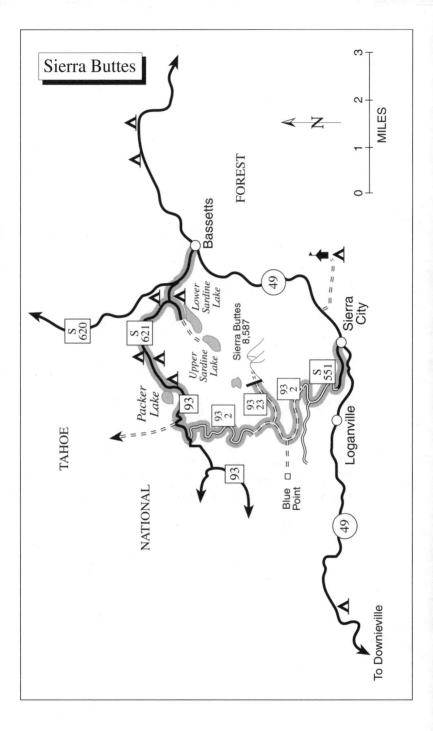

Sierra Buttes

Diggins I

LOCATION: Tahoe and Plumas National Forests, between Downieville at the south end and La Porte at the north end.

HIGHLIGHTS: This tour will take you through the rugged northern gold mine regions, where mountains were scarred by hydraulic mining. Sights include old mining sites, historic buildings and gold camps from the mid 1800s to 1884. The northern Sierra vista from the lookout atop 6,690-foot Saddleback Mountain is outstanding. You can link up with Diggins II (Tour 2). The Gold Rush town of Downieville is worth a visit as well.

DIFFICULTY: Easy to moderate. 4WD Poker Flat Road (800) is steep and can be muddy. Do not ford Canyon Creek during high water. These roads can be closed by storms.

TIME & DISTANCE: 3 hours; 29 miles.

MAPS: Tahoe National Forest or Plumas National Forest.

INFORMATION: Plumas National Forest, Feather River Ranger District; Tahoe National Forest, Downieville Ranger District.

GETTING THERE: To go north (the way I take you)**:** Take Hwy. 49 to Cannon Point, an overlook above the North Yuba River west of Downieville where there is indeed an old cannon. On the north side of the highway is Saddleback Road (509). Follow it north toward Poker Flat. **To go south:** From La Porte, take paved Quincy-La Porte Road (511) northeast for almost a mile, then turn right (east) onto unpaved St. Louis Road (512).

REST STOPS: Refer to your map for area campgrounds. There are primitive campsites at Poker Flat, Howland Flat and Yankee Hill. The Saddleback Mountain Lookout is a great place to stop.

THE DRIVE: At Cannon Point you can gaze into the valley of the North Yuba River. Below is Downieville, named for Maj. William Downie, a Scot whose party of miners found gold here in 1849. Saddleback Road (509) climbs on a shelf above the valley, then bends north. At a junction at mile 7.7 from Hwy. 49, keep to the right and continue ahead, toward Saddleback Lookout and Poker Flat. 0.4 mile farther, the spur to the lookout branches right (east). This rough road provides more views of craggy Sierra Buttes (Tour 1), and ends in 0.6 mile. Continue toward Poker Flat. The road passes Mt. Alma and Democrat Peak, and in a few miles it descends steeply to the ford at Canyon Creek. Near Poker Flat, go left at the Y, and continue through diggings. Cross the creek to reach Poker Flat, at the junction of Saddleback and Poker Flat roads. Poker Flat was the hub of a rich hydraulic mining district. Poker Flat Road (800) climbs steeply, then descends to the site of Potosi. Go left (west) at the fork and follow road 690 through Howland Flat (there is a cemetery on the south side of the road). The road crosses land that was devastated by hydraulic mining. 4.8 miles from Howland Flat, take the road that descends to the right, toward Yankee Hill. On St. Louis Road, you'll pass a bridge built in 1913, then reach pavement east of La Porte.

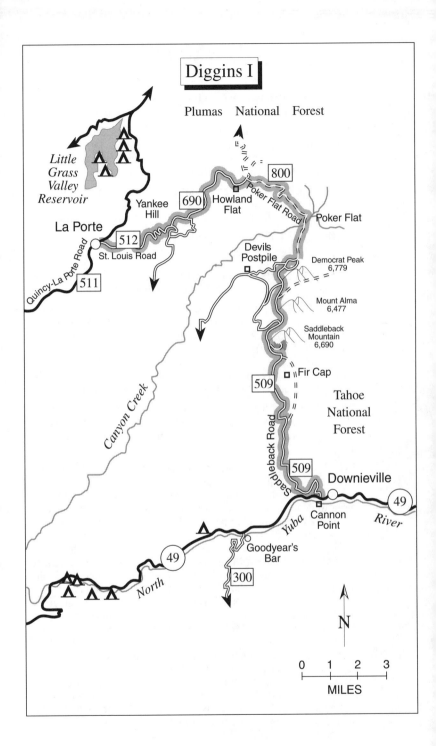

Diggins I

Plumas National Forest

Little Grass Valley Reservoir

800

690   Howland Flat   Poker Flat Road   Poker Flat

Yankee Hill

La Porte   512

Quincy-La Porte Road   St. Louis Road

511

Devils Postpile   Democrat Peak 6,779

Mount Alma 6,477

Saddleback Mountain 6,690

509   Fir Cap

Tahoe National Forest

Saddleback Road

509   Downieville

49

Cannon Point   River

Yuba

Canyon Creek

Goodyear's Bar

49   North   300

N

0   1   2   3

MILES

Diggins II

LOCATION: Between Goodyear's Bar (on Hwy. 49) at the north end, and Nevada City (also on Hwy. 49) at the south end.

HIGHLIGHTS: This tour combines northern Sierra scenery with historic sites like Nevada City, Malakoff Diggins State Historic Park, North Bloomfield, Alleghany, Forest City and Goodyear's Bar, early North Yuba River mining camps.

DIFFICULTY: Easy overall, but rocky and narrow in places. Storms and slides can close the roads, particularly just north of the Middle Yuba River. There are many junctions to keep track of.

TIME & DISTANCE: 3.5 hours; 48 miles.

MAP: Tahoe National Forest.

INFORMATION: Tahoe National Forest, Downieville and Nevada City ranger districts. Malakoff Diggins SHP.

GETTING THERE: From Nevada City (as described): Take Hwy. 20, then go west on Hwy. 49. Soon you'll see the Forest Service office (check road conditions). Just west of it, turn north onto North Bloomfield Road (522). Zero your odometer. **From Goodyear's Bar:** 4 miles west of Downieville on Hwy. 49, turn south onto Goodyear Creek Road; cross the river on the old bridge, then follow Mountain House Road (S300) south.

REST STOPS: Nevada City and Downieville have services. There are campgrounds at the South Yuba River and Malakoff Diggins. North Bloomfield has restrooms, picnic area, and cabins.

THE DRIVE: Paved, narrow and serpentine North Bloomfield Rd. forks half a mile from the highway. Go right, toward North Bloomfield. At mile 6 it enters the South Yuba River Recreation Area and descends to a bridge over the South Yuba River. Pavement ends here. Climb out of the gorge, then go right at mile 8.7, toward North Bloomfield. At mile 11.2, at Lake City Road, go right again. At mile 11.3 the road enters the park, where you can view the Malakoff Mine, where hillsides were hosed away. A lawsuit ended hydraulic mining in 1884. Soon you will reach old North Bloomfield, Malakoff's supply center. Stay on road 522. About 3.7 miles from North Bloomfield is a junction; go right (east), toward Graniteville for a half-mile. Then turn left (north) at another junction, and follow the little road to Buck's Ranch and Moore's Flat. 1.9 miles from that turn, make a hard right onto a small road. It will descend to Moore's Flat and Buck's Ranch. 0.8 mile from the ranch, the road (833) bends right, but your route is the 4x4 trail ahead that plunges into Gold Canyon. In a mile, at a junction, keep left. At the Middle Yuba River angle right, across rock to a bridge. Beyond the river is a sign indicating whether the road ahead is open. (It's often left in the "closed" position regardless of conditions.) Road S200 climbs, bends south then north, and arrives at a junction on Lafayette Ridge. Go north through Chips Flat. The road crosses another bridge. Go left at a Y; continue to Alleghany and Pliocene Ridge Rd. (S180). Cross the latter, and take Mountain House Rd. (S300) north to historic Forest City and Hwy. 49 (10 miles).

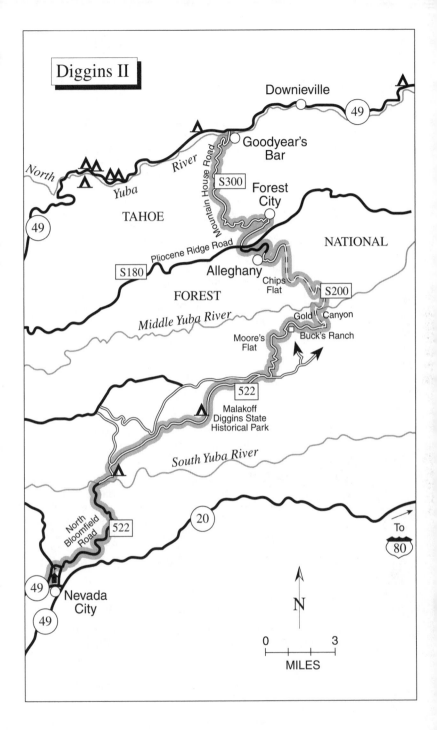

Diggins II

Downieville

49

Goodyear's Bar

S300

North

Yuba River

TAHOE

Mountain House Road

Forest City

49

Pliocene Ridge Road

NATIONAL

S180

Alleghany

FOREST

Chips Flat

S200

Middle Yuba River

Gold Canyon

Moore's Flat

Buck's Ranch

522

Malakoff Diggins State Historical Park

South Yuba River

North Bloomfield Road

522

20

To

80

49

Nevada City

49

N

0   3

MILES

Henness Pass Road

LOCATION: Between Verdi, Nevada, and California Hwy. 49, Tahoe National Forest. The east end is in Toiyabe NF.

HIGHLIGHTS: This east-west road over Henness Pass, said to be the last trans-Sierra backcountry road, is named for Patrick Henness, who developed the pass in 1849 or 1850 into a Gold Rush-era route. With the discovery of the Comstock Lode in 1859 at Virginia City, Nevada, it became the main route between there and Marysville. Declining mine production and the completion of the transcontinental railroad in 1869 reduced use to local traffic. Near the west end, at the confluence of Oregon Creek and the Middle Yuba, drive through the Oregon Creek covered bridge (ca. 1862). East of Camptonville is Sleighville House, a Gold Rush-era stage stop. Side trips go to the old mining towns of Forest City and Alleghany. West of Jackson Meadow Res. the road follows a ridge between the North and Middle Yuba rivers, providing excellent views, particularly of Sierra Buttes (Tour 1). At Kyburz Flat there are rock-art sites. At the east end, drive up 8,444-foot Verdi Peak.

DIFFICULTY: Easy, on asphalt, gravel, dirt and rock. Although remote in places, it's pretty much a high clearance 2WD road.

TIME & DISTANCE: 6 hours and 90 miles with the 13.7-mile (round-trip) spur to Verdi Peak. It can be taken in segments.

MAPS: Tahoe NF. CSAA's *Feather River & Yuba Regions.*

INFORMATION: Downieville and Sierraville Ranger Districts. The brochure *A Historic Driving Tour of the Henness Pass Road* explains 22 sites beginning at Hwy. 49.

GETTING THERE: To go east: Take Hwy. 49 north from Nevada City to the Oregon Creek bridge, then to Camptonville. There, follow Cleveland Avenue east uphill to Henness Pass Road. **To go west:** Take I-80 to Verdi, Nevada. Take Bridge Street to Dog Valley/Henness Pass Road. Take Dog Valley/ Henness Pass Road to a Y, at the turnoff to Dog Valley via Long Valley Road. At the Y, Henness Pass Road (860) is the left branch.

REST STOPS: Oregon Creek Day Use Area. See the map for campgrounds. Kyburz Flat has toilets and an interpretive trail.

THE DRIVE: From Camptonville, take graveled road 293 along a ridge to Mountain House Road (S300). There, you can detour to historic Forest City and Alleghany, then backtrack to road S302, a dirt leg of Henness Pass Road, or take the paved segment (Pliocene Ridge Road) east to the dirt portion. This ridgecrest segment (S301), west of Jackson Meadow Reservoir, is the roughest part. It's also where you will cross the pass. It joins paved Henness Pass Road (07) at the lake's northwestern corner. East of Webber Lake, where the Webber Lake Hotel was built in 1860, and west of Hwy. 89, the route makes a short detour to the south bank of the Little Truckee River. There is a great 360-degree vista from Verdi Peak Lookout.

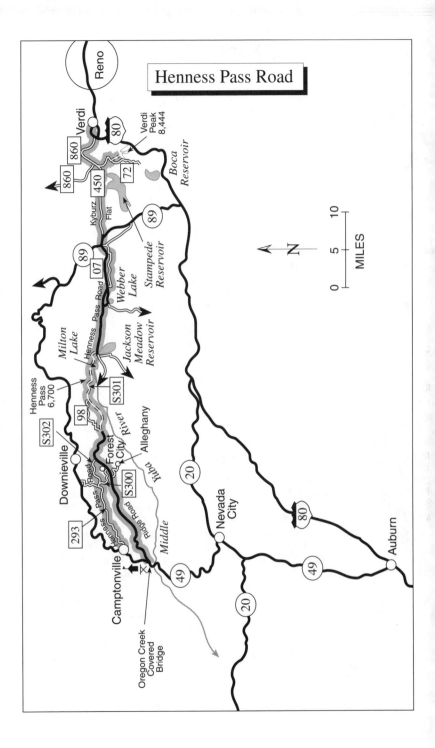

Henness Pass Road

Grouse Ridge/Bowman Lake

LOCATION: Tahoe National Forest. Between Hwy. 49 and Interstate 80. North of Yuba Gap.

HIGHLIGHTS: This drive winds through a spectacular landscape that includes numerous lakes, high cliffs, canyons, a historic town site and cemetery, an awesome 360-degree vista from the 7,707-foot-high Grouse Ridge Lookout (built in 1923), and mountain biking, hiking, canoeing, fishing and camping opportunities. All of it lies within easy reach of Reno, Sacramento and the Bay Area.

DIFFICULTY: The first 10.2 miles of Bowman Lake Road are paved. The unpaved roads are easy but a bit rough.

TIME & DISTANCE: There's so much to see that I suggest making this a two-day camping trip. Plan on driving upwards of 70 miles, including 5.3-mile (one-way) Grouse Ridge Road, or even more depending on which of the side roads you explore.

MAPS: Tahoe National Forest. CSAA's *Feather River and Yuba Regions*.

INFORMATION: Tahoe National Forest, Nevada City and Sierraville ranger districts.

GETTING THERE: Take U.S. 20 southwest for about 3.7 miles from its junction with I-80 at Yuba Gap (Yuba Pass on some maps). Turn north onto Bowman Lake Road (18).

REST STOPS: There are developed campgrounds in the area, as well as many primitive campsites. Refer to your map.

THE DRIVE: From Hwy. 20, Bowman Lake Road (18) winds north through forest and soon crosses the South Fork of the Yuba River at Lang Crossing. Then it climbs through a granite canyon to bring you to the Grouse Ridge Road (14) turnoff 6.3 miles from the highway. Go right (east) through the gate, and follow Grouse Ridge Road to a campground, the sparkling lakes of Grouse Lakes Basin, and a fire lookout that provides an inspiring vista of the northern Sierra and beyond. Bowman Lake is about 9 miles north of the Grouse Ridge Road turnoff. At its western end you will see Bowman House, owned by the Nevada Irrigation District. Cross the bridge over Canyon Creek, and soon you will come to Meadow Lake Road (843). Go right (east). Meadow Lake Road goes more or less east along the northern edge of Bowman Lake to pretty Meadow Lake and the site of once-bustling Summit City. Founded in 1862 by H.W. Hartley, it had 5,000 people in 1864. But the gold that sparked the boom proved too difficult to extract, and the city soon died. Hartley's resting place is well-marked in the old cemetery. East of the lake is the turn left (north) on road 86 toward Webber Lake and paved Henness Pass Road (Tour 4; shown as Fiberboard Road on the CSAA map). The latter will take you 9 miles east to Hwy. 89. (The 10-mile round-trip spur to White Rock Lake, which is nice but can be buggy, may not be worthwhile if time is limited.)

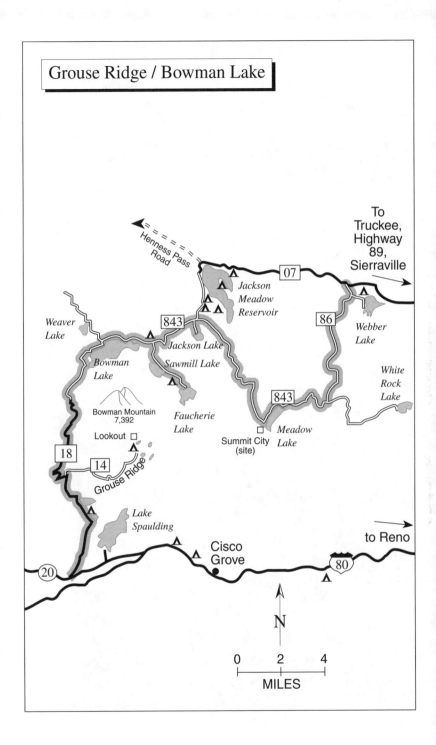

Grouse Ridge / Bowman Lake

To Truckee, Highway 89, Sierraville

Henness Pass Road

Jackson Meadow Reservoir

07

86

Webber Lake

843

Weaver Lake

Jackson Lake

Sawmill Lake

White Rock Lake

Bowman Lake

843

Bowman Mountain 7,392

Faucherie Lake

Meadow Lake

Summit City (site)

Lookout

18

14

Grouse Ridge

Lake Spaulding

Cisco Grove

to Reno

20

80

N

0   2   4
MILES

Cemetery at Howland Flat (Tour 2)

Colfax-Foresthill Bridge, North Fork of the American River (Tour 6)

Iowa Hill Loop

LOCATION: Placer County, on the North Fork of the American River east of Colfax and I-80.

HIGHLIGHTS: You will edge along beautiful canyons and mountainsides that are still recovering from 19th century hydraulic gold mining, and cross the North Fork of the American River on a rare single-lane suspension bridge built in 1930.

DIFFICULTY: Easy, though narrow and serpentine. Iowa Hill Road, and a mile of Yankee Jim's Road, are paved.

TIME & DISTANCE: 1.5 hours; 24 miles.

MAPS: Tahoe NF. CSAA's *Feather River and Yuba Regions*.

INFORMATION: Placer County.

GETTING THERE: This loop begins and ends at I-80. I start at Colfax. Exit I-80 at Colfax/Hwy. 174. On the east side of the interstate (which is going north and south here), take Canyon Way south from the overpass for 0.3 mile. Turn left onto Iowa Hill Rd. Reset your odometer. To go the opposite way, starting farther south on I-80, take the Auburn St. exit to Canyon Way. Take Canyon Way south for 0.7 mile. Turn left onto Yankee Jim's Rd.

REST STOPS: Mineral Bar CG, at the river on Iowa Hill Rd. There's river access and a toilet at the Colfax-Foresthill Bridge.

THE DRIVE: It didn't take long for the "easy" gold to be taken from the Sierra's rivers and streams during the Gold Rush. To extract the gold that lay inside the mountains, in ancient riverbed gravels and sediments, mining companies used high-pressure streams of water to wash away entire mountainsides. You can still see eroded hydraulic mining sites in places like the Iowa Hill District, around the bygone town of the same name. Gold was discovered here in 1853. Three years later weekly production was estimated at $100,000. By 1880, the district had produced $20 million in gold. From today's I-80, Iowa Hill Rd. plunges into the canyon of the North Fork of the American River, where there's an old suspension bridge that is now just a foot bridge. Then the narrow road climbs to Iowa Hill Divide, at mile 8.6. You can see hydraulic mining sites on either side. A bit farther is the site of Iowa Hill, destroyed several times by fire. You can see the remains of a vault that once stood inside a Wells Fargo Express Office. (The town of Yankee Jim's stood west of Foresthill, on Yankee Jim's Rd.) Follow the signs for Yankee Jim's, Foresthill and Shirttail Canyon. Keep right at a junction at mile 11.2, and follow unpaved Shirttail Canyon Road down into Shirttail Canyon (named for a miner found working only in a shirt). This enchanting road winds along to Yankee Jim's Rd., at mile 17.6. Go right past an old mine addit and waterfall. Soon you will reach the old Colfax-Foresthill Bridge. Beyond are more addits, evidence of the drift mining that came after hydraulic mining was banned in 1884. From there you will climb again, reaching pavement in 3.6 miles, and Canyon Way 1.1 miles farther. You'll reach I-80 soon thereafter.

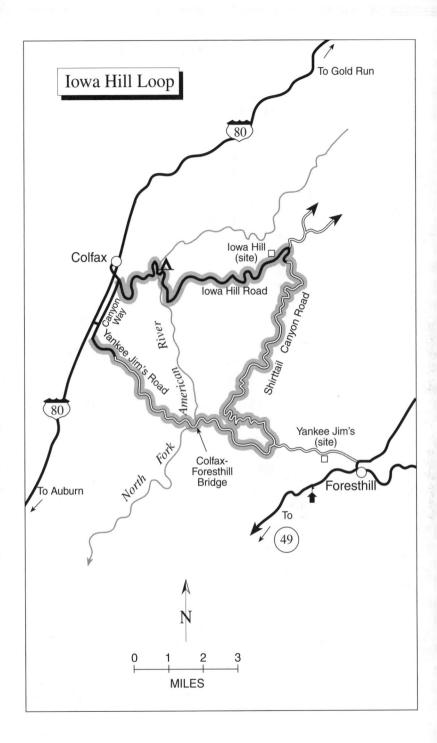

Iowa Hill Loop

To Gold Run

80

Colfax

Iowa Hill (site)

Iowa Hill Road

Canyon Way

Yankee Jim's Road

American River

Shirttail Canyon Road

North Fork

Colfax-Foresthill Bridge

Yankee Jim's (site)

To Auburn

Foresthill

To 49

N

0   1   2   3
MILES

Blue Canyon-Ross Crossing

LOCATION: Northeast of Fresno. Sierra National Forest, between Pine Flat and Wishon reservoirs

HIGHLIGHTS: This loop will take you along Blue Canyon, through forest to pretty Haslett Basin and on through granite-strewn High Sierra scenery. High points, including Fence Meadow Lookout, provide terrific vistas if the smog isn't too bad.

DIFFICULTY: Easy, on a mix of unpaved and paved road segments. Note: The Dinkey-Trimmer Road (10S69) is closed from December 12 to May 20 for wildlife protection.

TIME & DISTANCE: 3 hours; 59 miles.

MAP: Sierra National Forest.

INFORMATION: Sierra NF, Pine Ridge Ranger District.

GETTING THERE: Take Hwy. 168 northeast to Shaver Lake. Go east on Dinkey Creek Road. About 9 miles east of Shaver Lake (and about 3 miles west of Dinkey Creek), turn south onto Providence Creek Road, road 10S17 & No. 9 (it's mistakenly labeled No. 7 on older Sierra National Forest maps).

REST STOPS: You will find developed and undeveloped campsites along the way, as well as numerous places to stop for a break. Gas, food and lodging are available at Dinkey Creek.

THE DRIVE: Providence Creek Road descends through forest to Blue Canyon and the junction with Big Creek Road. Go left (south), following Big Creek Road (still road 9) past Bretz Campground and the Blue Canyon Work Station. About 4.2 miles south of the junction the road narrows to a ledge and then descends into pretty Haslett Basin. Here you will reach the junction with Dinkey-Trimmer Road. You can go south, to Pine Flat Reservoir in about 8 miles, and on to Hwy. 168 and Fresno. The tour continues winding south on Dinkey-Trimmer Road (10S69), so go left at the junction. Soon the road crosses Nutmeg Creek, and then climbs out of the basin, providing outstanding vistas to the south and west. Almost 5 miles from the last junction is a gate that closes the road for wildlife protection. The serpentine road will bend north, and take you to the turnoff (road 11S08) to Fence Meadow Lookout, which provides a typical panoramic view. 3.6 miles from here is the junction at Nutmeg Saddle. The tour goes right, onto road 10S40 to road 10S24, Ross Crossing Road. This narrow road descends to another intersection in 4.3 miles; keep right on Ross Crossing Road. It will wind down into another deep canyon and cross Dinkey Creek on a bridge at Ross Crossing, a gorgeous place to stop, have lunch or camp. From here the road climbs again, entering an open area with exposed granite, including the dome of Black Rock. Farther on lies Ross Meadow. The drive continues north to end at paved McKinley Grove Road (40), about 9 miles southeast of Dinkey Creek.

Blue Canyon – Ross Crossing

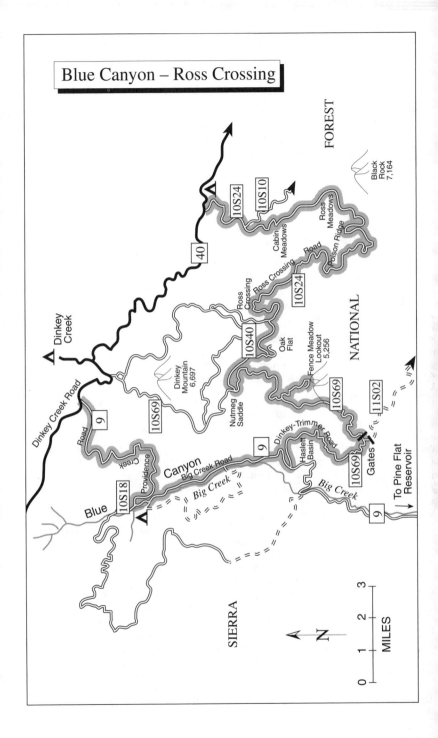

TOUR
8

Black Rock Road

LOCATION: East of Fresno, between Wishon and Pine Flat reservoirs. Sierra National Forest.

HIGHLIGHTS: This is a gorgeous drive on a narrow shelf road high above the canyon of the North Fork of the Kings River. The segment above Granite Gorge is particularly impressive. Though it's an easy drive (more than half of this route is paved), you will edge along sheer drop-offs on one-lane segments that cross tiny bridges in two places. There are many vista points, and you will see a number of huge Pacific Gas & Electric penstocks, dams and other power-generating facilities.

DIFFICULTY: Easy, though narrow and serpentine.

TIME & DISTANCE: 2.5 hours; about 28.5 miles.

MAP: Sierra National Forest.

INFORMATION: Sierra National Forest, Pine Ridge & Kings River Ranger Districts.

GETTING THERE: From the Fresno area, make your way east on Trimmer Springs Road to the eastern end of Pine Flat Reservoir. Turn north across the South Fork of the Kings River, toward the town of Balch Camp.

REST STOPS: There are developed campgrounds and other recreation facilities along the South Fork of the Kings River, at Black Rock and Wishon reservoirs, and at Sawmill Flat.

THE DRIVE: The paved road takes you through Balch Camp, then angles east to climb higher into the mountains, the source of the waters that run the hydroelectric plants here. About 0.4 mile from Balch Camp, the road passes beneath the Dinkey Creek siphon. A couple of miles farther, as you hug the canyon wall above the North Fork of the Kings River, you will cross the first of two hair-raising one-lane bridges, and beyond them pass beneath the Balch Penstocks. Eventually you will reach the turnoff for PG&E's Black Rock Reservoir and campground, named for a 7,164-foot peak to the north. The pavement on this winding road ends in another 1.6 miles, at the gated turnoff to the Haas Powerhouse, but the unpaved segment ahead is maintained and easily driven. Beyond that, however, is a particularly narrow segment, and more stunning views of the gorge below. A few miles farther, high above fantastic Granite Gorge and just before you reach Sawmill Flat Campground, the road forks. The main road, 11S12, continues for 3.5 miles to paved McKinley Grove Road (Forest Hwy. 40). Take the right branch, road 11S01, a spectacular shelf road at the head of Granite Gorge that will cross a saddle, pass a small lake and, 4.5 miles from the turnoff, deliver you to Wishon Reservoir.

Black Rock Road

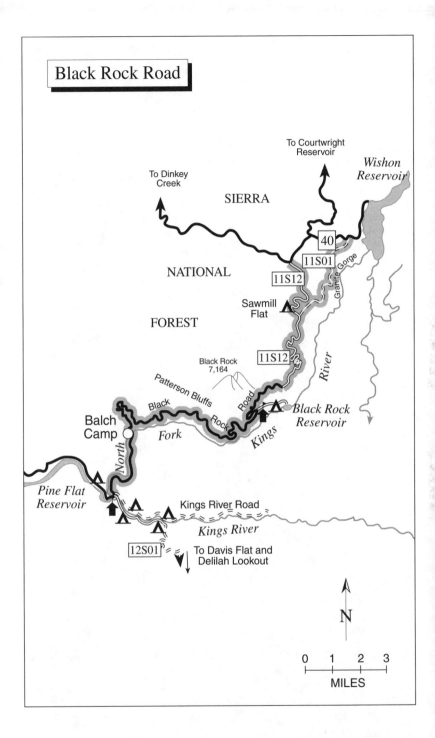

To Courtwright Reservoir

Wishon Reservoir

To Dinkey Creek

SIERRA

40

11S01

11S12

NATIONAL

Granite Gorge

Sawmill Flat

FOREST

River

Black Rock
7,164

11S12

Patterson Bluffs

Black Rock Road

Balch Camp

Black

Rock

Black Rock Reservoir

Fork

Kings

North

Pine Flat Reservoir

Kings River Road

Kings River

12S01

To Davis Flat and Delilah Lookout

N

0   1   2   3

MILES

Granite Gorge (Tour 8)

Deer Creek Drive (Tour 10)

Delilah Lookout – Kings River

LOCATION: East of Fresno, between Black Oak Flat (Hwy. 180) and the South Fork of the Kings River. Sequoia National Forest.

HIGHLIGHTS: You will have sweeping vistas across the southern Sierra along this drive, but none will come close to the panorama at Delilah Lookout, which stands atop 5,156-foot Delilah Mountain. (The lookout is a terrific destination by itself.) The northern segment parallels the beautiful South Fork of the Kings River.

DIFFICULTY: Easy.

TIME & DISTANCE: 3.5 hours; about 30 miles, including the 12-mile side trip to Delilah Lookout.

MAPS: Sequoia National Forest. ACSC's *Tulare County*.

INFORMATION: Sequoia NF, Hume Lake Ranger District.

GETTING THERE: From Fresno, take Hwy. 180 east into Sequoia National Forest. At Black Oak Flat, turn left (north) at the sign for Delilah Lookout.

REST STOPS: There are three developed campgrounds and an undeveloped campground and picnic area at the north end, along the river. Delilah Lookout is a great place to stop.

THE DRIVE: From Hwy. 180, take paved forest road 12S01 north to the intersection with road 12S19, which goes east where 12S01 goes north (you'll return to this junction). Eventually 12S19 will bend northwest and climb to Pine Ridge. When you reach a fork almost 3 miles from where 12S01 and 12S19 split, take the left branch, road 13S75. The ridgeline road, steep and loose in some places, provides numerous inspiring vistas of the Central Valley to the north and west and deep canyons to the east. About 1.8 miles from the last fork, the road drops to the left, but the lookout is a short distance ahead. After visiting the lookout, return to 13S75, and follow it north for a short distance, then go right (east), on 12S19 again. It loops around the east side of Delilah Mountain, then angles south to return you to the junction with 12S01, which you want to take north along the western edge of the Kings River Special Management Area, toward Sampson Flat and the South Fork of the Kings River. It will climb to Goat Saddle, then snake along a ledge as it descends among rugged canyons to Davis Flat, where it follows Davis Creek through Crabtree. The road will bend west when it reaches the river at Mill Flat. Soon you will come to a steel bridge across the river, which is the end of the drive. You can continue west to Pine Flat Reservoir. For more adventure, cross the river and take scenic but dead-end Kings River Road along the north bank. Or take terrific Black Rock Road (Tour 8) along the North Fork of the Kings River in Sierra National Forest.

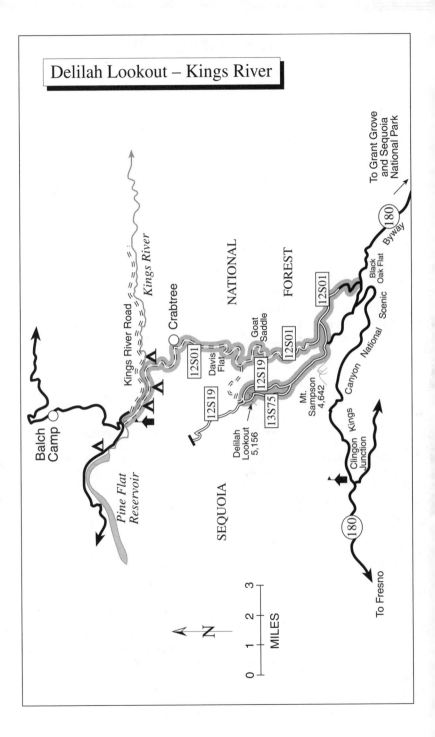

Delilah Lookout – Kings River

To Grant Grove
and Sequoia
National Park

180
Byway

Black
Oak Flat

12S01

NATIONAL

Kings River

Crabtree

FOREST

Goat
Saddle

12S01

Kings River Road

12S01

Davis
Flat

12S19

12S19

13S75

Mt.
Sampson
4,642

Canyon National Scenic

Delilah Lookout
5,156

Clingon Kings
Junction

Balch
Camp

Pine Flat Reservoir

SEQUOIA

180

To Fresno

N

MILES

0   1   2   3

Deer Creek Drive

LOCATION: Tulare County, southeast of Porterville.

HIGHLIGHTS: You just might find yourself trailing behind a cattle drive on this tour through a bucolic landscape that seems a precious remnant of California from the early 1900s. The serene beauty of oak woodlands, rocky hills of golden grass and the canyon and valley of Deer Creek combine to make this little mountain road one of the prettiest in the foothills of the southern Sierra. You can combine this with Old Hot Springs Road (Tour 11).

DIFFICULTY: Easy, on a narrow 2WD dirt road.

TIME & DISTANCE: 1 hour; 18.2 miles.

MAP: ACSC's *Tulare County.*

INFORMATION: Tulare County.

GETTING THERE: From the south (the way I describe it): At Fountain Springs (north of Bakersfield) take paved Hot Springs Road east toward California Hot Springs. In 7 miles you can detour onto the Old Hot Springs Road (a.k.a West Old Control Drive/M-52) tour by turning left (north). Just follow it for 10.8 miles to where it rejoins Hot Springs Road. Then go left (northeast) for about 0.4 mile. Where Hot Springs Road bends east, go north onto Tyler Creek Road. Just across Tyler Creek, angle left (west) onto Deer Creek Drive. **From the north:** Make your way to Magnolia (north of Bakersfield and south of Porterville), and then to Avenue 120. Follow it west, and it will become M (or MTN) 120, which will bend north to become Road 296. Just north of the bend, turn east onto Deer Creek Drive, also called Deer Creek Road (M-112).

REST STOPS: Sequoia National Forest's Leavis Flat Campground, just across the forest boundary off Hot Springs Road.

THE DRIVE: From the south, this narrow, one-lane mountain road, a genuine bit of bygone California where you almost expect to encounter a bouncing stagecoach or chugging Model T, twists along a canyon wall high above Deer Creek, with a sheer drop-off to the left. If you look south across the canyon, you will see Old Hot Springs Road/West Control Drive edging along the canyon as well. Deer Creek Drive eventually crosses a ridge, then drops into a valley and crosses Deer Creek. The pastoral valley's hills and fields are strewn with countless granite boulders and outcrops, and oaks are everywhere. About 16 miles from Hot Springs Road, Deer Creek Drive widens, and the steep Sierra foothills you traveled through earlier have diminished to lower, gentler hills. At about mile 18.1 you will reach paved road MTN 120 south of Porterville.

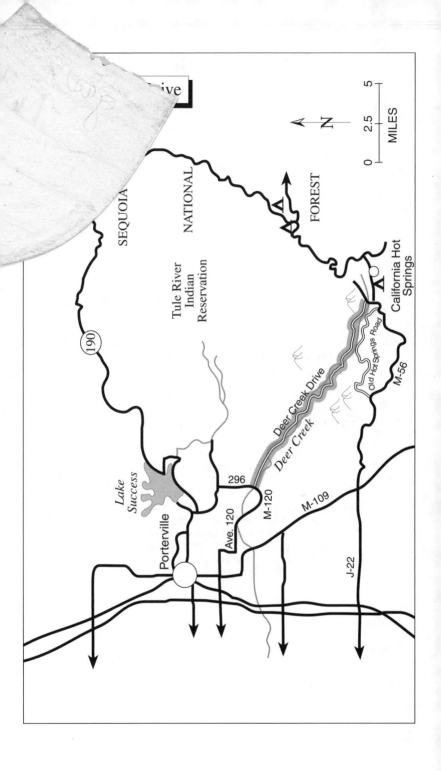

TOUR
11

Old Hot Springs Road

LOCATION: Tulare County, southeast of Porterville.

HIGHLIGHTS: This is a thrilling, highly scenic and serpentine old shelf road high on the wall of a canyon in the foothills of the southern Sierra. You can make a terrific loop by combining this with nearby Deer Creek Drive (Tour 10).

DIFFICULTY: Easy, on a 2WD dirt road.

TIME & DISTANCE: 40 minutes; 10.8 miles.

MAP: ACSC's *Tulare County*.

INFORMATION: Tulare County.

GETTING THERE: From Fountain Springs (north of Bakersfield), the way I describe below: Take Hot Springs Road east for 7 miles, then turn left (north) onto Old Hot Springs Road, a.k.a. Old Control Drive and MTN 52. **From Porterville:** Take beautiful Deer Creek Drive to Hot Springs Road. Take Hot Springs Road west for about 0.4 mile, then turn right (north) onto Old Hot Springs Road/Old Control Drive, and take the tour in the opposite direction from my description.

REST STOPS: The Sequoia National Forest Leavis Flat Campground is just across the forest boundary off Hot Springs Road.

THE DRIVE: Early on, a sign advises travelers that they are embarking on a narrow, winding road, and that is indeed true. It starts out crossing a flat expanse covered with scrub oak and grasses. After a mile or so it begins a gentle climb. To the west is a great view of the Central Valley, and ahead rise rugged Sierra foothills. By mile 3.7 the road has become a mere single-lane ledge supported in places by some interesting masonry work. The road twists along the southern wall of the canyon of Deer Creek. If you want to peer over the edge, stop and get out, lest you become part of the scenery down there yourself. By mile 10.7 you're on safer ground, and a short distance farther you're back on paved Hot Springs Road.

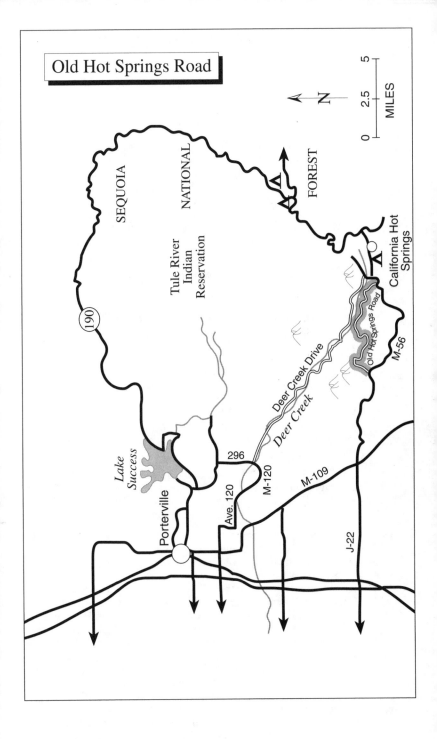

Old Hot Springs Road

Rancheria Road

LOCATION: Northeast of Bakersfield and west of Lake Isabella, in the Greenhorn Mountains of the southern Sierra. It extends between Hwys. 178 at the south end and 155 at the north end. The northern section is in Sequoia National Forest.

HIGHLIGHTS: This scenic backroad climbs (or descends, if you go south) through pastoral remnants of old California, amid rolling foothills, oak woodlands and pine forests, with views into the canyon of Kern River. Oak Flat Lookout, built in 1934, provides vistas of the Kern River, Greenhorn Mountains and San Joaquin Valley. Evans Flat, named for 19th century entrepreneur Robert Henry Evans, was a seasonal home for Indians for thousands of years. You can still see the holes where they ground acorns.

DIFFICULTY: Easy, on a maintained 2WD road.

TIME & DISTANCE: 3 hours; 37.5 miles.

MAPS: Sequoia National Forest. ACSC's *Kern County*.

INFORMATION: Sequoia National Forest, Greenhorn Ranger District. Greenhorn Summit Ranger Station, at the north end.

GETTING THERE: From the south (as described): Take Hwy. 178 (Kern Canyon Road) east from Bakersfield. About 3 miles east of the Hwy. 178/184 junction, turn left (north) at a large orchard onto Rancheria Road (465), paved at this end for 4.2 miles. **From the north:** Take Hwy. 155 (Forest Road 210) to Greenhorn Summit (west of Lake Isabella). Turn south onto Rancheria Road.

REST STOPS: The Oak Flat Lookout can be rented for overnight stays (contact the Greenhorn Ranger District). Evans Flat Campground is pleasant, but waterless. There's camping at Kern County Park, at the north end at Greenhorn Summit.

THE DRIVE: Pavement ends in 4.2 miles, after winding north from Hwy. 178 into treeless hills. The road takes you through oak woodlands dotted with old ranch buildings and granite outcrops. You were at about 820 feet above sea level, but after 11 miles you will have climbed above 3,000 feet. The views of the Central Valley are outstanding. The road narrows to a single lane and once again climb steeply. Almost 15 miles from Hwy. 178 is the short spur to Oak Flat Lookout (the road is closed at a gate in 0.4 mile; you have to walk the rest of the way). Beyond that is a view of the Kern River. Rancheria Road comes to an intersection; continue north toward Evans Flat and Hwy. 155. Beyond that is the boundary of Sequoia National Forest, and a junction. Continue north to a Y, stay on road 465 (25S15) toward Greenhorn Summit. About 28.5 miles from Hwy. 178 is Evans Flat Campground. where you can view the bedrock mortars. For thousands of years, the Tabatulabal Indians came here to gather plants and hunt. A short distance on is the junction with Sawmill Road. In about 5 miles you'll reach pavement at Shirley Meadows. Hwy. 155 is 2.4 miles farther, beyond an overlook above Lake Isabella.

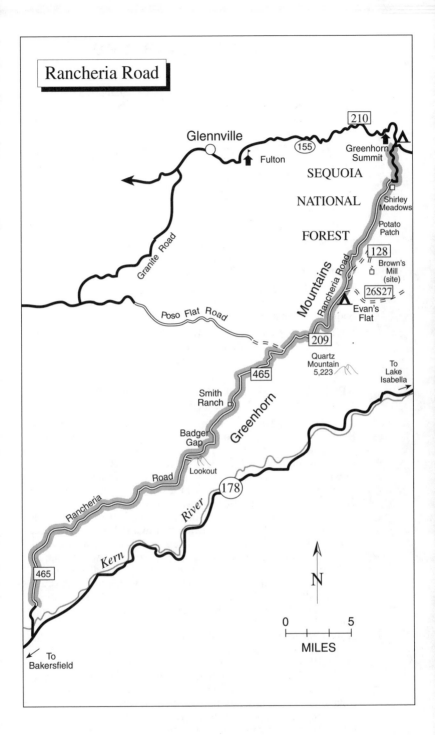

Rancheria Road

Jawbone to Lake Isabella

LOCATION: In the Piute Mountains of the southern Sierra; east of Bakersfield and north of Tehachapi. Between Hwy. 14 south of Red Rock Canyon State Park and Bodfish, near Lake Isabella. Sequoia National Forest.

HIGHLIGHTS: You will experience the transition from the Mojave Desert to the forests of the rugged southern Sierra as you climb from 2,500 feet to over 8,000 feet. The descent to Kern Valley and Bodfish via a narrow shelf road is spectacular.

DIFFICULTY: Easy.

TIME & DISTANCE: 3 hours; 53 miles.

MAPS: Sequoia National Forest. ACSC's *Kern County*. At Jawbone Station get a copy of *East Kern County Off-Highway Vehicle Riding Areas & Trails*.

INFORMATION: BLM's Jawbone Station information center, near the junction of Jawbone Canyon Road and Hwy. 14. Sequoia National Forest, Greenhorn Ranger District.

GETTING THERE: From Hwy. 14 about 1.2 miles south of Red Rock-Randsburg Road (18 miles north of Mojave), take the Jawbone Canyon/Kelso Valley exit. Follow Jawbone Canyon Road west.

REST STOPS: BLM's Jawbone Station. You will find all services at Bodfish and Lake Isabella.

THE DRIVE: Drive west through the Jawbone Canyon Off-Highway Vehicle Area on Jawbone Canyon Road (589). The pavement will end about 4.1 miles from Hwy. 14 after you pass two large pipelines of the Los Angeles Aqueduct. Ahead is a green-blue hill, Blue Point. It marks the entrance to Alphie Canyon, which you'll reach at mile 4.7. From there the route climbs into semi-arid mountains, providing outstanding vistas across the Mojave Desert before bringing you to Butterbredt Canyon Road (SC123). Continuing toward Kelso Valley on Jawbone Canyon Road, the hills become dotted first with Joshua trees, then pinyon pines and junipers (later on, oak woodlands and the typical conifer forests of the Sierra), signaling a transition between climate zones. Soon the road descends into pastoral Kelso Valley, to the junction with Kelso Valley Road at about mile 17.8. Go west through the junction, following the sign for Piute Mountain. Jawbone Canyon Road will bend south and cross a meadow. The road then turns west and climbs into the Piute Mountains, passing through oak woodlands. From there you will ascend the steep and narrow switchbacks of the Geringer Grade and enter Sequoia National Forest. Continue north to the junction with Piute Mountain Road (501) and forest road 27S02 (the latter is labeled Saddle Spring Road on the Forest Service map, but is Piute Mountain Road on the CSAA map). When you reach the junction, at about mile 31.1, take 27S02 left (west). It will make a thrilling descent to paved Caliente-Bodfish Road (483), in Kern Valley just south of Bodfish.

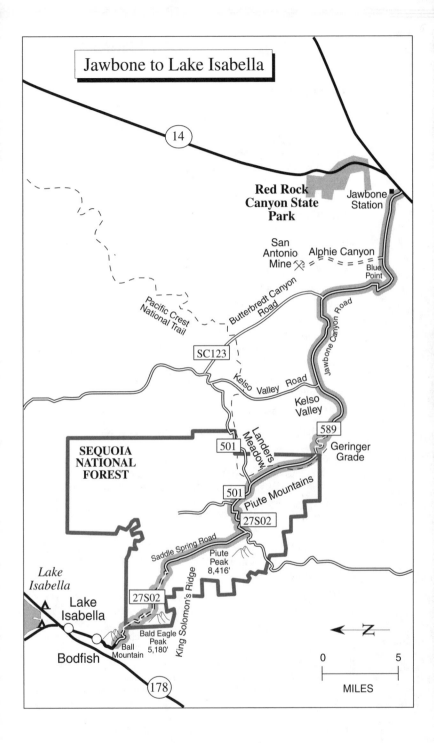

Jawbone to Lake Isabella

Chimney Peak Byway

LOCATION: The tour circles Chimney Peak in the southern Sierra, near Sequoia National Forest between Kennedy Meadow Road and Hwy. 178, northeast of Lake Isabella.

HIGHLIGHTS: This tour of southern Sierra Nevada wildlands follows one of the BLM's National Back Country Byways. It loops around 7,990-foot Chimney Peak, passing through more than 50,000 acres of federally designated wilderness in a transition zone between the Sierra Nevada and the Mojave Desert.

DIFFICULTY: Easy. The BLM classifies this a Class II byway of narrow, slow-speed secondary roads suitable for high-clearance vehicles. Segments of the southern portion of Long Valley Loop Road are paved. Unpaved segments can be washboarded. Some sections may be impassable in winter and early spring.

TIME & DISTANCE: 2.5 to 3 hours and 44 miles, beginning and ending at Hwy. 178. About 1.5 hours and 25 miles for Long Valley Loop Road, beginning and ending at Nine Mile Canyon Road.

MAPS: Sequoia National Forest. ACSC's *Tulare County*. Bring the BLM's flyer, *Chimney Peak Back Country Byway; A passage through changing times*, which explains points of interest. You may find some at the kiosk on Canebrake Road just off Hwy. 178.

INFORMATION: BLM's Bakersfield Field Office.

GETTING THERE: From the south (the way I describe it): Take Hwy. 178 to Canebrake Road (20 miles east of Lake Isabella, and 18 miles west of Hwy. 14). Turn north onto Canebrake Road. **From U.S. 395:** Take the Kennedy Meadow turnoff (32 miles south of Olancha), and follow Nine Mile Canyon Road west for 11.7 miles. Turn left (west) onto unpaved Long Valley Loop Road where the paved road bends north and becomes Kennedy Meadow Road.

REST STOPS: Long Valley Campground, off Long Valley Loop Road, and Chimney Creek Campground, along Canebrake Road. Neither has water.

THE DRIVE: Serpentine Canebrake Road climbs along mountainsides above South Fork Valley and Chimney Creek. To the west is the Domeland Wilderness; to the east is the Owens Peak Wilderness. There are turnouts where you can take in the vistas, but don't expect guardrails. In about 9 miles you will come to the junction with the almost 20-mile-long Long Valley Loop Road, an even narrower and twistier mountainside road that makes a spectacular loop high above Long Valley between the Domeland and Chimney Peak wildernesses, coming out at Kennedy Meadow Road. You can take it now, or continue winding north to Kennedy Meadow Road and take the loop road in the opposite direction. Either way, the two ends of the unpaved byway are about 0.5 mile apart via Kennedy Meadow Road. The scenery and solitude along this lonely backroad is superlative no matter which way you go.

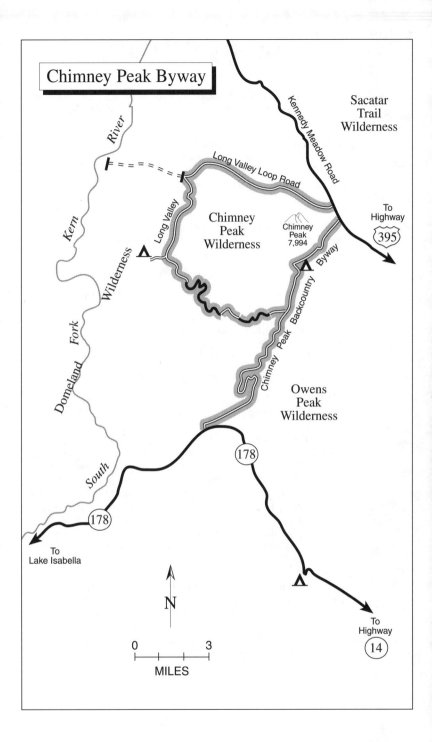

Chimney Peak Byway

Sacatar
Trail
Wilderness

Kennedy Meadow Road

River

Long Valley Loop Road

Kern

Long Valley

Chimney
Peak
Wilderness

Chimney
Peak
7,994

To
Highway

Wilderness

Fork

Domeland

Chimney Peak Backcountry Byway

395

Owens
Peak
Wilderness

South

178

178

To
Lake Isabella

N

Owens
Peak
Wilderness

To
Highway

14

0   3

MILES

Cherry Hill Road

LOCATION: Sequoia National Forest, north of Lake Isabella, west of the Domeland Wilderness and south of Sherman Pass Road.

HIGHLIGHTS: This pleasant cruise takes you through high, picturesque mountain meadows flanked by granite peaks and forest. The side trip to the Brush Creek overlook provides outstanding vistas across the southern Sierra.

DIFFICULTY: Easy.

TIME & DISTANCE: 2 hours and 37 miles round-trip to Big Meadows. There are areas to explore south of Big Meadows that can add another hour or two.

MAPS: Sequoia National Forest. ACSC's *Tulare County*.

INFORMATION: Sequoia NF, Cannell Meadow Ranger District.

GETTING THERE: Take Sherman Pass Road east for 4.7 miles from the junction with Sierra Way (Kern River Road). Turn south onto Cherry Hill Road (22S12).

REST STOPS: Horse Meadow Campground.

THE DRIVE: Much of the pleasure of this drive lies in getting to it, because Sherman Pass Road is just spectacular. Cherry Hill Road, which is paved for the first 5.7 miles, follows Poison Meadow Creek south through a forested area watered by numerous small streams. Almost 2 miles from where the pavement largely ends, the road to scenic Brush Creek overlook (23S14) branches left (northeast). This narrow dirt road ends in almost 3 miles, at a turnaround area. Park there, and walk through the trees to a rocky knoll from which you can gaze out at the rugged mountain expanse. From this turnoff, Cherry Hill Road continues south past its 8,833-foot-high namesake, which stands east of the road, and Horse Meadow, where you'll find a developed campground. From here it descends into a landscape dotted with granite, and eventually you will see Big Meadow and the prominent summit of 9,470-foot Cannell Peak. Continue to South Big Meadow Road, which makes a scenic 5.9-mile loop that returns to Cherry Hill Road, passing two trailheads leading into the Domeland Wilderness. This is as far as I take you, but you can continue south to Long Meadow, Cannell Meadow, Rattlesnake Meadow and the logged region called Bartolas Country.

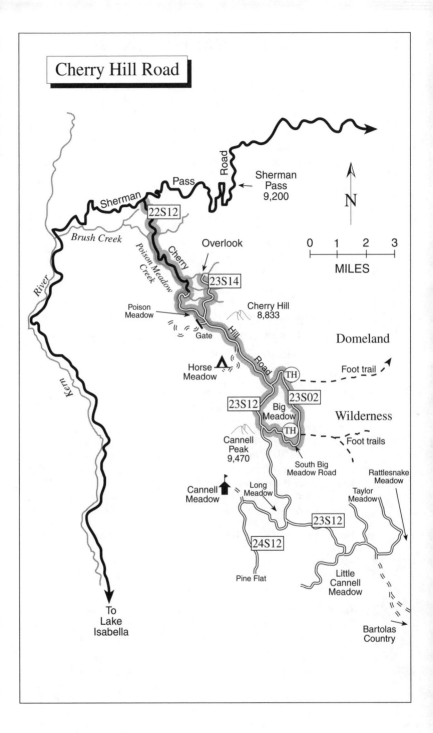

Cherry Hill Road

Sherman Pass
9,200

N

0 1 2 3
MILES

Brush Creek

River

Kern

22S12

Cherry

Poison Meadow Creek

Overlook

23S14

Cherry Hill
8,833

Domeland

Foot trail

Poison
Meadow

Gate

Hill

Road

Horse
Meadow

TH

23S12

23S02

Big
Meadow

Wilderness

TH

Foot trails

Cannell
Peak
9,470

South Big
Meadow Road

Cannell
Meadow

Long
Meadow

Rattlesnake
Meadow

Taylor
Meadow

23S12

24S12

Little
Cannell
Meadow

Pine Flat

Bartolas
Country

To
Lake
Isabella

Monache Meadows

LOCATION: Southwest of Olancha (on U.S. 395), along the South Fork of the Kern River, in Inyo National Forest (although you have to pass through Sequoia National Forest to get there). It's bordered on the west and north by the Golden Trout Wilderness, and on the east by the South Sierra Wilderness.

HIGHLIGHTS: Six miles long, five miles wide and more than 8,000 feet high, Monache Meadows is often cited as the largest mountain meadow in the Sierra. Almost surrounded by wilderness and drained by the wild and scenic South Fork of the Kern River, it is a remote and popular destination. It lacks the grandeur of granite peaks, but makes up with a ring of low mountains, streams and meadows. Anglers can try their luck fishing for German brown and hybrid golden/rainbow trout.

DIFFICULTY: Easy to moderate. The road is narrow and in places requires maneuvering between trees. The South Fork of the Kern River, just a stream here, may be deep in early summer. The route usually opens to motor vehicles by July.

TIME & DISTANCE: 4-5 hours; about 25 miles round-trip from where the pavement ends.

MAPS: Sequoia NF. USGS' *Monache Mountain* topo map.

INFORMATION: Inyo National Forest, Mt. Whitney Ranger Station. The Blackrock Work Station.

GETTING THERE: From the east: Take the Kennedy Meadows turnoff from U.S. 395 (32 miles south of Olancha), onto Nine Mile Canyon Road. Follow the signs for Sequoia National Forest's Blackrock Work Station (37 miles), to the junction with Sherman Pass and Blackrock roads (Nine Mile Canyon Road will become Kennedy Meadow Road). **From the west:** Take Sherman Pass Road northeast to the junction with Kennedy Meadow Road, near the work station. **From the junction**: Drive north on Blackrock Road (21S03) about 3.5 miles. Turn right (east) onto paved road 21S36, at the sign for the Monache Meadows 4WD road (a.k.a. Sherman 4WD Trail). At the Y in 3.5 miles, go left (north) through the gate. The pavement ends here. Set your odometer to 0.

REST STOPS: There are primitive campsites in Monache Meadows, and two developed campgrounds (Troy Meadow, Fish Creek and Kennedy Meadows) along Kennedy Meadow Road.

THE DRIVE: The road through a forest of fir and pine is well-maintained for the first mile. Beyond a pack train staging area, the route turns into a rocky, undulating 4WD trail that climbs and descends. At about mile 1.4 you may encounter a rough section. At mile 2.6 is a ledgy section to crawl down as you enter Bull Meadow. Just beyond a gate, ford Snake Creek and enter Inyo National Forest. Round a bend to the east. Monache Meadows appears ahead. From here the road over Summers Ridge to the meadows and the river ford is obvious.

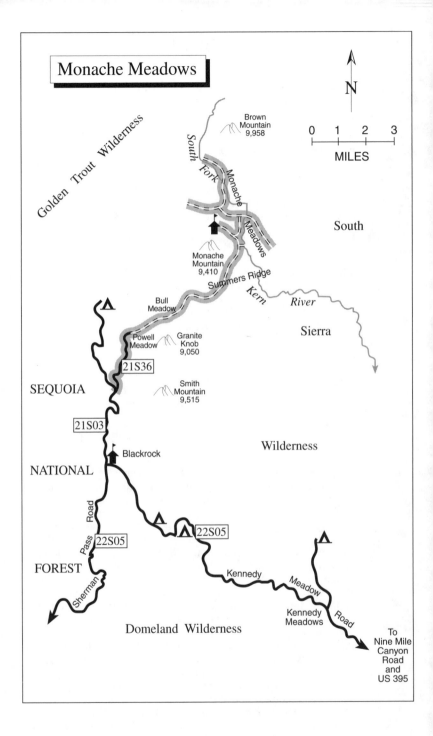

Monache Meadows

N

Golden Trout Wilderness

Brown
Mountain
9,958

0 1 2 3
MILES

South
Fork
Monache
Meadows

South

Monache
Mountain
9,410

Summers Ridge

Kern

River

Sierra

Bull
Meadow

Powell
Meadow

Granite
Knob
9,050

21S36

Smith
Mountain
9,515

SEQUOIA

21S03

Wilderness

NATIONAL

Blackrock

22S05

22S05

FOREST

Kennedy

Meadow

Road

Pass Road

Sherman

Kennedy
Meadows

Domeland Wilderness

To
Nine Mile
Canyon
Road
and
US 395

Alabama Hills

LOCATION: At the base of the eastern Sierra below Mt. Whitney, in the Owens Valley west of Lone Pine.

HIGHLIGHTS: Alabama Hills is a jumbled expanse of huge, rounded, honey-brown granite boulders with one of the Sierra's most spectacular backdrops: the peaks of the Muir Crest, which culminate at 14,495-foot Mt. Whitney, the highest point in the contiguous states. This region has been a favorite stage for movie makers and advertisers since the 1920s, and is popular for photography and rock climbing. Wildflowers add to this convenient drive during the first two weeks or so of May.

DIFFICULTY: Easy on the graded main roads. Some spurs can be rougher.

TIME & DISTANCE: About an hour and 13 miles for the loop north of Whitney Portal Road, or more if you explore the spurs.

MAPS: Inyo National Forest. ACSC's *Eastern Sierra*.

INFORMATION: BLM, Bishop Field Office. Interagency Visitor Center, south of Lone Pine at the junction of U.S. 395 and Hwy. 136.

GETTING THERE: From U.S. 395 at Lone Pine, take Whitney Portal Road west, directly toward the mountains, for 2.7 miles. Turn right (north) onto Movie Road.

REST STOPS: Fuel, food and lodging are available in Lone Pine. There also are a number of campgrounds in the area; refer to your map. Dispersed camping in the Alabama Hills is discouraged.

THE DRIVE: The 30,000-acre, BLM-managed Alabama Hills Recreation Area is a landscape of dramatic contrasts. Soaring to the west are the snow-salted peaks and spires of the eastern Sierra, sculpted by glaciers and the effects of water freezing and thawing in the granite's cracks and crevices. The Alabama Hills, however, consist of massive jointed and faulted boulders. They are almost identical in age (80 million years) and composition to the mountains behind them, but are thought to have been shaped by chemical weathering when the climate was wetter and the rocks were buried. In 1862, a dark precursor of the many fictional Western shootouts filmed here occurred when settlers attacked a Paiute Indian camp, killing 11. When some Confederacy sympathizers found gold here, they named their claims the Alabama District, after the Confederate Navy cruiser *Alabama*, which sank 64 Union merchant ships during the Civil War. Union sympathizers countered by naming their mining district, a town east of Independence (along Mazourka Canyon Road), a mountain and a pass after the Union's *Kearsarge*, which sank the *Alabama* in June 1864 off the port of Cherbourg, France. Beginning in the 1920s, Hollywood made the Alabama Hills familiar to moviegoers as the setting for numerous Westerns and other films. Thus, the road initially crosses an open area that has starred in so many films it's been dubbed Movie Flat.

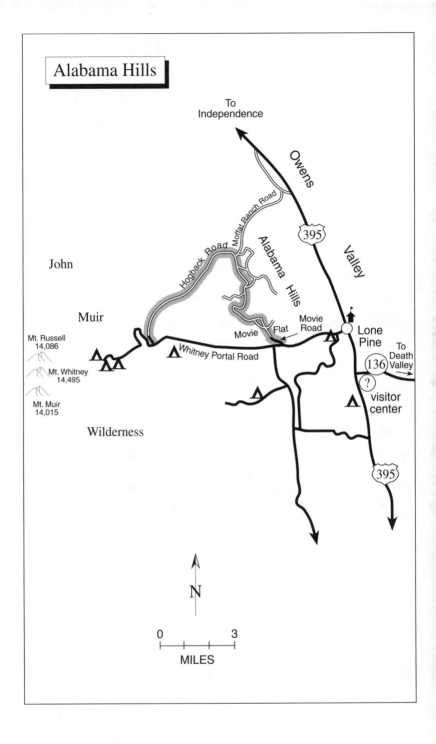

Alabama Hills

To Independence

Owens Valley

395

John

Muir

Mt. Russell
14,086

Mt. Whitney
14,495

Mt. Muir
14,015

Wilderness

Hogback Road

Moffat Ranch Road

Alabama Hills

Whitney Portal Road

Movie Flat

Movie Road

Lone Pine

To Death Valley

136

? visitor center

395

N

0 ——— 3
MILES

Inyo Mountains

LOCATION: East of the Sierra Nevada, in Inyo County. With the geologically linked White Mountains (Tour 20), the Inyo Mountains form the eastern wall of the 10,000-foot-deep Owens Valley. You will start at Independence, and exit to the north at Death Valley Road (a.k.a. Saline Valley/Eureka Valley Road), east of Big Pine. This route links up with Tour 19 at Papoose Flat.

HIGHLIGHTS: Although not as high as the Sierra Nevada, these desert mountains provide a spectacular and exhilarating driving experience. In addition to canyons, ridges and flats, you will have terrific vistas across the Owens Valley to the Sierra, especially from Mazourka Peak and Papoose Flat.

DIFFICULTY: Easy to moderate. Start at Independence and go north so you can descend the rough segment leading to Papoose Flat. There are short sidehill sections.

TIME & DISTANCE: 7-8 hours. It's about 64 miles from Independence to Big Pine, including Santa Rita Flat and Mazourka Peak. You will see many appealing spurs to explore.

MAP: Inyo National Forest.

INFORMATION: Inyo National Forest, Mt. Whitney Ranger Station. Eastern Sierra Visitor Center, at Hwys 395 & 136 just south of Lone Pine.

GETTING THERE: Just south of Independence, go east toward the mountains on Mazourka Canyon Road (13S05) from U.S. 395.

REST STOPS: There are primitive campsites at Badger Flat and elsewhere. No water or facilities are available.

THE DRIVE: At the base of the mountains, veer left (north), following dirt Mazourka Canyon Road (13S05) up the scenic gap, which is unusual in that it runs north-south instead of the more typical east-west. At mile 12.3 is the left (west) turn for road 13S05A to Santa Rita Flat, which has a great vista. About 18.1 miles from U.S. 395 is Badger Flat; keep left. In another mile is a right fork that you will follow later. Keeping left, follow a small road (11S01) up to an awesome view from 9,412-foot Mazourka Peak. Return to that right fork you saw earlier, and angle northeast past a corral. About 0.1 mile beyond the ruins of Blue Bell Mine, go left. Climb a steep section toward a saddle. Just after going down a dip, you will see a small Y. Descend on the left track. Cross two sidehills, then descend to a small valley. Note the track to the northwest (left) from the valley floor; that's your route, road 9S15. In 2.3 miles the road may seem to vanish, but it's to the left. Descend a rough section, then continue to Papoose Flat, an important food-gathering place for Native Americans for thousands of years. Follow 9S15 north across Papoose Flat (joining Tour 19). Keep right at the Y just beyond the junction with road 10S07, cross the broad flat and descend via switchbacks to Death Valley/Saline Valley/Eureka Valley Road. Big Pine is about 13 miles to the left (west), via Hwy. 168.

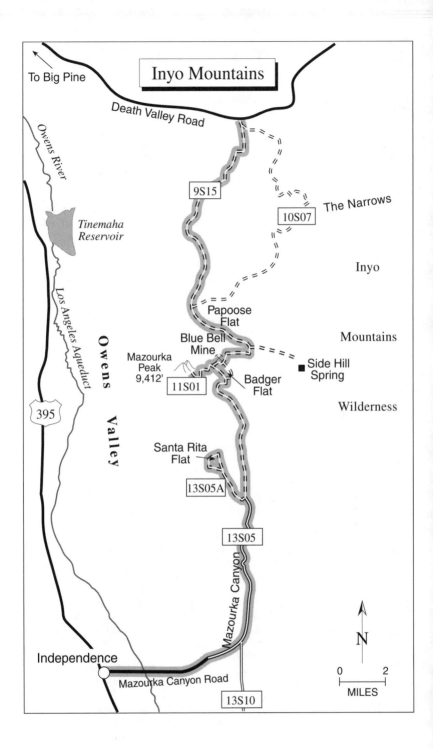

The Narrows – Papoose Flat

LOCATION: Inyo Mountains, southeast of Big Pine.

HIGHLIGHTS: You will wind through a narrow canyon on a single-lane road that passes an even narrower, high-walled cleft, The Narrows. Papoose Flat is a high expanse marked by countless large granite outcrops (including one with an arch). It provides a fantastic view across the Owens Valley to the Sierra. This route connects with Tour 18, Inyo Mountains.

DIFFICULTY: Easy. The canyon is rocky and sandy in places. Avoid the dangerous old mine addits. The route is well-marked.

TIME & DISTANCE: 3.5 hours; 25.5 miles.

MAP: Inyo National Forest.

INFORMATION: Inyo NF's Mt. Whitney Ranger Station.

GETTING THERE: Take Hwy. 168 east from U.S. 395 at Big Pine. In 2.2 miles turn right (southeast) onto paved Death Valley Road (a.k.a. Saline Valley Road and Big Pine to Death Valley Road). In another 11.2 miles turn right (south) at the sign for Papoose Flat. In 0.1 mile you will come to a Y, the start of the loop. Set your odometer to 0. From here you can go in either direction. The left branch (9S14) takes you into a long canyon, then to Papoose Flat. The southbound branch (9S15) provides a more direct and earlier view of the Sierra .

REST STOPS: There are no services beyond Big Pine. There are many primitive campsites, but no developed campgrounds.

THE DRIVE: Either direction of this loop has advantages. From the Y at the start, the left (eastward) branch (9S14) follows the bottom of a long, rocky ravine. It climbs gradually for about 3.7 miles to a divide, then descends to a narrow, meandering canyon. About 3 miles from the divide, at a left spur marked by some old mine buildings, is the entrance to The Narrows. This high-walled gap of dark, laminated rock (schist) is worth a short hike. From there the road becomes 10S07 as it continues south to Squaw Flat along the western boundary of the Inyo Mountains Wilderness. About 2 miles from The Narrows is a 4-way junction; go left (right, if you're going in the opposite direction). In a mile, where road 9S14 branches left, keep right, and soon you will enter an area of granite boulders much like the jointed and faulted rocks at more famous Alabama Hills (Tour 17). Papoose Flat, a food-gathering place for Indians for thousands of years, is just ahead. Keep an eye out for a large rock island just north of the road where erosion has formed an arch. Less than a mile farther is the junction with road 9S15 (which climbs south as a 4WD road to Badger Flat, Tour 18). Take in the view of the Sierra, then go right (north), then right again at the small Y. The road crosses Papoose Flat, then descends via switchbacks to the Y at the start of the loop. If you go in the opposite direction at the outset, the southbound (right) branch (9S15) climbs the switchbacks to Papoose Flat, where you go left (east) on 10S07 toward The Narrows.

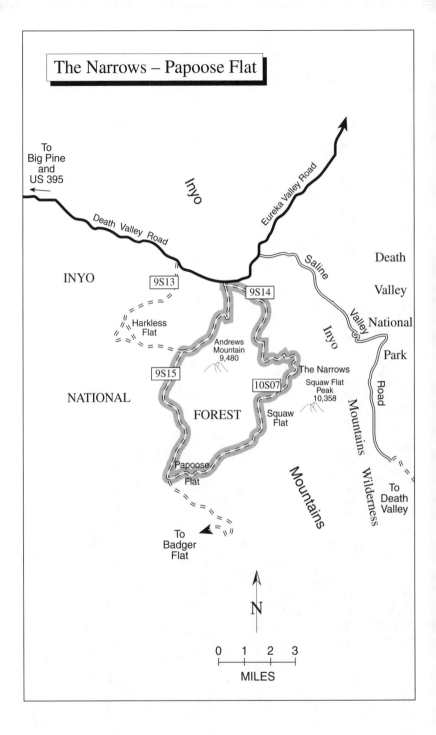

The Narrows – Papoose Flat

Papoose Flat (Tour 19)

Silver Canyon Road, White Mountains (Tour 20)

White Mountains

LOCATION: Inyo National Forest, east of Bishop and U.S. 395.

HIGHLIGHTS: Between the soaring peaks of the Sierra and the Whites lies the 10,000-foot-deep Owens Valley. The Whites provide great views of the Sierra, but are most famous for ancient bristlecone pines. White Mountain Peak (14,246 feet) is California's third-highest. The drive climbs to about 11,680 feet.

DIFFICULTY: Easy overall. The 3.9 unpaved miles of narrow Silver Canyon Road (6S02) below the top is moderately difficult, particularly going uphill. It is steep and narrow with some tight switchbacks. The lower 6.5 miles to pavement are easy. It's best to go down it, because the driving is easier and you can enjoy the terrific views of Silver Canyon, the Owens Valley and the High Sierra. The roads atop the Whites are graveled and maintained. 10 miles of White Mountain Road from Hwy. 168 to Schulman Grove are paved.

TIME & DISTANCE: All day. It's about 68 miles from U.S. 395 at Big Pine to U.S. 395 at Bishop. The hike to White Mountain Peak is a strenuous, all-day 15-mile (round-trip) trek from the locked gate at the north end of the drive.

MAPS: Inyo National Forest. ACSC's *Eastern Sierra.*

INFORMATION: Inyo NF, White Mountain Ranger Station. Ancient Bristlecone Pine Visitor Center at Schulman Grove.

GETTING THERE: From Big Pine (going down Silver Canyon Road): Go northeast on Hwy. 168 toward Westgard Pass. 12.7 miles from Big Pine, turn north on White Mountain Road. **From Bishop** (going up Silver Canyon Road): About 3.8 miles north of town on U.S. Hwy. 6, turn east onto Silver Canyon Road.

REST STOPS: No water, fuel or services are available. Grandview Campground is 5.4 miles north of Hwy. 168 on White Mountain Road. Schulman Grove has the oldest known bristlecones, a visitor center, trails and a picnic area. Patriarch Grove has the largest known bristlecone, and picnic tables.

THE DRIVE: The well-watered and forested Sierra are generally composed of glaciated granite, an igneous rock, while the Whites are composed primarily of sedimentary rock 500 million to 600 million years old. Fossils nearly 600 million years old are found here. Standing in the rain shadow of the Sierra, the semiarid Whites lack the moisture necessary to form the kind of glaciers that bulldozed through the Sierra. The dry air leaves the Whites seemingly barren, but for their hardy, gnarled bristlecones, some of which are more than 4,600 years old. The Ancient Bristlecone National Scenic Byway, the road on the crest, winds through the Whites' rocky mountaintops. It ends at a locked gate at the north end. From there, at about 11,680 feet, hikers ascend to Mt. Barcroft Laboratory, a high-elevation research facility (1.9 miles), and White Mountain Peak.

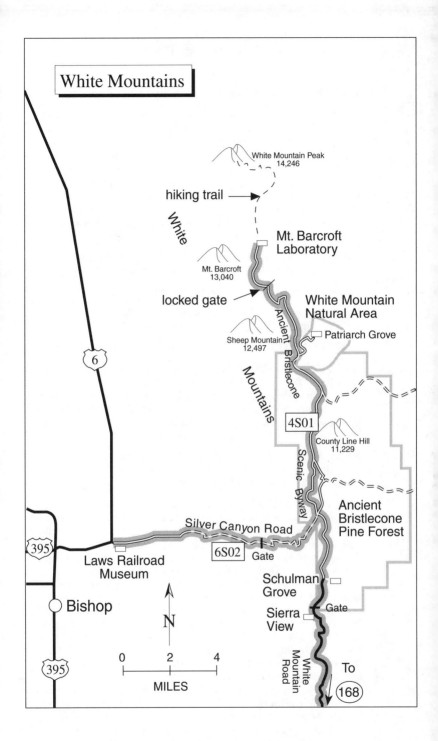

White Mountains

White Mountain Peak
14,246

hiking trail →

White

Mt. Barcroft
Laboratory

Mt. Barcroft
13,040

locked gate →

White Mountain
Natural Area

Ancient Bristlecone

Patriarch Grove

Sheep Mountain
12,497

Mountains

4S01

County Line Hill
11,229

Scenic Byway

Ancient
Bristlecone
Pine Forest

Silver Canyon Road

6S02 Gate

Laws Railroad
Museum

Schulman
Grove

Bishop

Sierra
View

Gate

N

White Mountain Road

0   2   4

MILES

To
168

§ 6

§ 395

§ 395

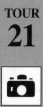

TOUR
21

Coyote Flat

LOCATION: Inyo National Forest southwest of Bishop.

HIGHLIGHTS: The drive goes from the desert Owens Valley to Coyote Flat, a vale more than 10,000 feet high below the Palisade Group's 13,000- to 14,000-foot peaks. The Sierra's second-highest cluster of peaks (after the Muir Group, which includes 14,495-foot Mt. Whitney), their steep slopes, sharp crest, small glaciers and perennial snowfields make them an inspiring alpine sight. The return has vistas across the 2-mile-deep Owens Valley to the White Mountains, highest in the Great Basin. You can hike to Baker Lake, in the John Muir Wilderness, from the Baker Creek trailhead. There are 4WD spurs to explore as well.

DIFFICULTY: Easy to moderate, with some particularly rocky spots. There also will be narrow sections and switchbacks.

TIME & DISTANCE: 6-7 hours; 50 miles.

MAPS: Inyo NF. ACSC's *Eastern Sierra*. Also useful are the USGS' *Coyote Flat* and *Mt. Thompson* topo maps.

INFORMATION: Inyo NF, White Mountain Ranger Station.

GETTING THERE: In Bishop, take West Line Street west for 1.5 miles. Turn left (south) onto South Barlow Lane. Go 0.1 mile. Turn right onto Underwood Lane. After 0.8 mile, where the road curves to the right, go left. Set your odometer at 0. Veer right just before the power substation. Go under the power lines and head into the mountains on Coyote Flat Road.

REST STOPS: There are many undeveloped but established campsites, including at Coyote Lake and the trailhead at Baker Creek, where there's an old pit toilet.

THE DRIVE: The road is sandy at first, then it passes through a ravine and climbs toward a canyon. At mile 3.9 is a branch to the right; keep left. The road becomes No. 7S10 when it enters the national forest, where it will be steep and rocky as it climbs through boulder-strewn canyons. You will pass a branch on the left at mile 10; continue on the main road. At mile 12.1 the road brings you to the left fork to Coyote Flat, Sanger Meadow and Baker Creek via road 7S10. You'll return to this later, but for now go straight, on road 8S18 past the old Salty Peterson Mine and along the west fork of Coyote Creek. At mile 14.6 the road forks. The left (south) fork goes a short distance to tiny Coyote Lake. The right fork (8S19) turns north at the base of Coyote Ridge. At the next fork 0.4 mile farther the road goes left (west) to a beautiful subalpine basin, and north up the western flank of Lookout Mountain to 11,000-foot Coyote Ridge. Back at the Coyote Flat turnoff, ford Coyote Creek. From there the road (7S10) is an easy cruise south across Coyote Flat to Baker Creek, with awesome views of angular peaks that exceed 14,000 feet, and Middle Palisade Glacier. The road ends in about 6.7 miles at a primitive camping spot at Baker Creek (there's a pit toilet), near the John Muir Wilderness boundary and the trail to Baker Lake.

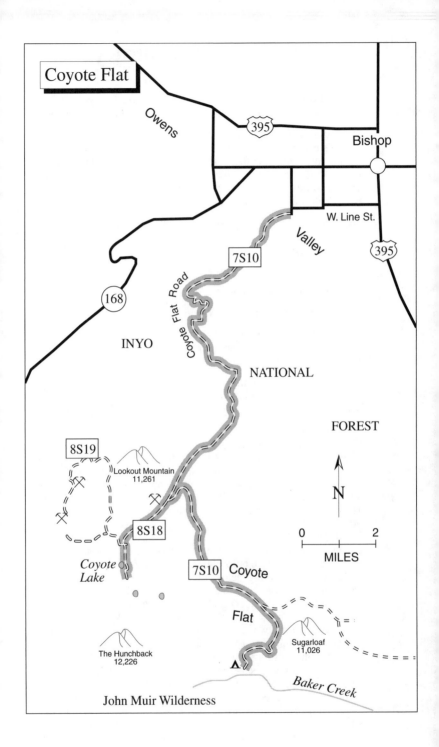

Buttermilk Country

LOCATION: West of Bishop. Most of it crosses Inyo National Forest land, but there are patches of land owned by Los Angeles.

HIGHLIGHTS: This drive takes you to the base of the eastern Sierra's escarpment, one of the steepest in the world, at the edge of the John Muir Wilderness. The views stretch from glaciated peaks more than 13,000 feet high across the 10,000-foot-deep Owens Valley to the White Mountains, which rise to over 14,000 feet. Buttermilk Country is popular for bouldering as well.

DIFFICULTY: Easy to moderate. Spurs are moderate to difficult.

TIME & DISTANCE: This is a 15-mile loop, or longer if you explore the many spurs. Allow 1.5-2 hours.

MAPS: Inyo National Forest. ACSC's *Eastern Sierra*.

INFORMATION: Inyo NF, White Mountain Ranger Station.

GETTING THERE: In Bishop, turn west from U.S. 395 (Main St.) onto West Line St. (Hwy 168). In about 7.3 miles, just into the national forest, turn onto unpaved Buttermilk Road (7S01).

REST STOPS: You will see many pleasant places to stop among the rocks, including primitive campsites. There are campgrounds south of Buttermilk Country as well. Bishop has all services.

THE DRIVE: I've heard two reasons for the name Buttermilk Country. One says teamsters from a sawmill on Birch Creek long ago would stop for a drink of buttermilk at a dairy. Another says that when 19th-century ranchers would haul goat milk to Bishop in the summer months, it would turn to buttermilk along the way. Today, visitors get to drink in some of the best of the eastern Sierra's inspiring grandeur. About 4 miles from Hwy. 168, after you pass through L.A.-owned Longley Meadow, Buttermilk Road diminishes to a single lane, and becomes rougher as it angles southeast and takes you gradually higher. If you've never felt dwarfed by nature before, bumping along this road should do it, for you are driving below the ramparts of such sentinels as Mt. Tom (13,652 feet), Basin Mountain (13,181 feet), Mt. Humphreys (13,986 feet) and Mt. Emerson (13,118 feet). The views of these peaks, and the canyons and rocky moraines left by glaciers, are awesome. Soon the road turns south behind Grouse Mountain, and passes through a relatively lush area. Then it's on through a stand of pines and aspens, a change from the vast expanses of sage-covered high desert. The road crosses McGee Creek, then makes a steep but short climb out of the creek's ravine. A rocky but worthwhile 4x4 spur, 8S17, branches to the right, and climbs to a basin in about a mile. Beyond this spur, Buttermilk Road crosses Birch Creek, then turns away from the mountains and begins the gradual descent along a narrow ridge overlooking the highway (which you will soon reach), and Bishop Creek Canyon, where the creek drops 400 feet per mile for 14 miles, generating electricity at several power plants.

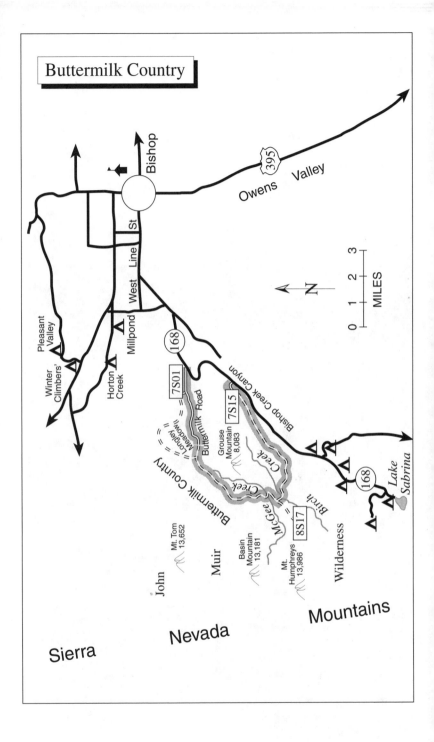

Buttermilk Country

Middle Palisade Glacier and Southfork Pass from Coyote Flat (Tour 21)

Buttermilk Country (Tour 22)

Volcanic Tableland

LOCATION: North of Bishop between U.S. 395 and U.S. 6, in the Owens Valley between the Sierra and the White Mountains.

HIGHLIGHTS: Like so many other locales along the Sierra's eastern slope (Mammoth Lakes, the Hot Creek Geologic Site, etc.), this high-desert expanse provides further evidence that this is indeed a quintessential land of fire (volcanic and geothermal forces) and ice (glaciers). The Volcanic Tableland, a popular place for bouldering, includes petroglyphs, the scenic gash of Red Rock Canyon and views of the Sierra's dramatic eastern escarpment. The old Casa Diablo Mine is interesting as well.

DIFFICULTY: Easy to moderate.

TIME & DISTANCE: 50 miles; 3.5 hours.

MAP: Inyo National Forest.

INFORMATION: BLM's Bishop Field Office.

GETTING THERE: I start at Bishop, but you can go the opposite way, beginning at Tom's Place on U.S. 395 northwest of Bishop. **From Bishop:** Take U.S. 6 for 1.4 miles. Turn left (north) onto Five Bridges Road. Drive 2.4 miles, through a gravel yard. After crossing a canal, turn right (north) onto Fish Slough Road (3V01).

REST STOPS: There are no facilities along the drive. Bishop has all services. Visitors, including climbers, are asked to use the BLM's year-round Climbers' Winter Campground, or Horton Creek and Pleasant Valley campgrounds.

THE DRIVE: This semi-arid landscape formed 700,000 years ago when volcanic vents to the northwest spewed clouds of hot rhyolitic ash and rock particles that fused into rock formations. In about 3 miles, Fish Slough Road will go past a wetland that supports plants and animals with water from the only natural springs remaining on the floor of the Owens Valley. About 6.9 miles from your turn onto Fish Slough Road, pull into the parking area to the left, walk to the rocks ahead and visit the grinding holes and petroglyphs. Four miles farther you'll see (on the right after you drop into Chidago Canyon) more petroglyphs behind a protective wire fence. There are more in another 5.9 miles, on the rocks to the left (west). In another 0.4 mile, go left (west) at the intersection, onto road 3S53. Soon you will enter narrow Red Rock Canyon. When the road exits the canyon and reaches an intersection marked CHIDAGO LOOP, go straight for 2.7 miles, then turn left (east) onto road 4S41, which soon becomes a somewhat rough single-lane road as it climbs uphill. When you reach a saddle and you're facing the White Mountains, go right, and follow the road down a rocky section. After another 1.2 miles you will reach an intersection with the two-track road to Casa Diablo Mine (an early-20th century gold mine) and road 3S02. From here, you can drive southeast for 19 miles to Bishop on easy 3S02, Casa Diablo Road. Better yet, take 3S02 north for 6.4 miles through a pretty canyon to Benton Crossing Road. Turn left (west) toward the Sierra, then south on 4S02 toward U.S. 395.

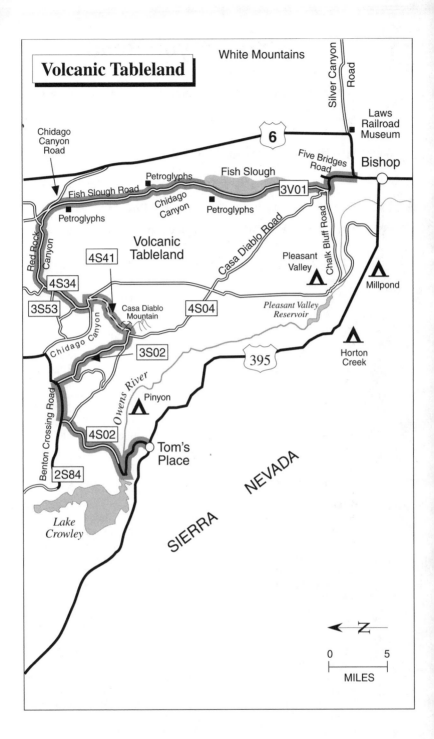

Sand Canyon Road

LOCATION: Inyo National Forest. The road runs along the eastern rim of Rock Creek Canyon northwest of Bishop and south of Tom's Place (on U.S. 395). It ends at the edge of the John Muir Wilderness.

HIGHLIGHTS: This drive provides outstanding views down into popular Rock Creek Canyon, and up at the John Muir Wilderness' chiseled, snowy peaks, which stand well over 13,000 feet. This is a popular downhill mountain-biking route as well. You can link it with Wheeler Ridge Road (Tour 25).

DIFFICULTY: Moderate. There are some very rocky stretches. Brush extends into the roadway in some places as well.

TIME & DISTANCE: 2.5 hours and 18.6 miles round-trip, excluding time spent at the lake.

MAPS: Inyo National Forest. For greater detail bring the USGS' *Mt. Morgan* and *Toms Place* 7.5-minute topo maps.

INFORMATION: Inyo NF, White Mountain Ranger Station.

GETTING THERE: Take U.S. 395 north of Bishop, then take the Lower Rock Creek Road (a.k.a. Old Sherwin Grade Road) to Swall Meadows Road. Take Swall Meadows Road 0.6 mile, then turn right onto Sky Meadow Road. Follow Sky Meadow Road for 0.5 mile. At a gravel pit you will see a two-track road (4S54) on the right. Reset your odometer here, and take 4S54. In 0.7 mile it will cross Witcher Creek, then immediately bend left (west). Now you're on Sand Canyon Road (5S08).

REST STOPS: There is a very pretty unnamed lake at the end of Sand Canyon Road. Stop at the cafe and store at Tom's Place.

THE DRIVE: The road follows Witcher Creek to Witcher Meadow, then continues along Birch Creek into the the narrow V of Sand Canyon. The roadbed is a coarse granitic sand, not the soft desert or beach sand that can require airing down substantially. The road climbs through pine trees, aspen, and stretches of narrow brush. By mile 3.9 you're making a long, steep climb to the top of the canyon, at 4.4. There you can pause at a turnout to take in the stunning mountain vista at the head of Rock Creek Canyon. In another half-mile, stop to look over the brink of the canyon, a busy place in summer with campgrounds, picnic areas and trailheads. At mile 5.4 is one of a number of rocky stretches where low range will be helpful. (Remember to keep your tires on the high points to avoid scraping your vehicle's undercarriage.) The roadside brush is quite close here as well, so your vehicle might acquire a pinstripe or two. At mile 7 you can look up to your left at Wheeler Ridge, which can be crossed via Wheeler Ridge Road (a.k.a. Wheeler Crest Road & Wheeler Ridge Mine Road), a more challenging 4WD road (Tour 25) that branches left at mile 7.3. (It isn't on the Inyo National Forest map, but is on the *Mt. Morgan* USGS topo map.) At mile 8.8 is a rocky downhill pitch that will require care. You will be rewarded at mile 9.3, when you arrive at a tranquil lake with a terrific view of soaring peaks.

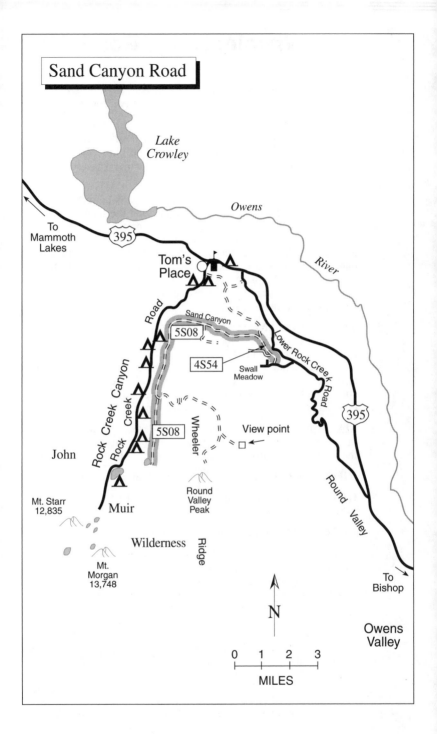

Sand Canyon Road

Lake Crowley

Owens

To Mammoth Lakes

395

Tom's Place

Road

Sand Canyon

5S08

River

Lower Rock Creek Road

4S54

Swall Meadow

Rock Creek Canyon

Wheeler

View point

395

Rock Creek

5S08

John

Round Valley Peak

Mt. Starr 12,835

Muir

Round Valley

Wilderness

Ridge

Mt. Morgan 13,748

To Bishop

N

Owens Valley

0   1   2   3

MILES

Wheeler Ridge Road

LOCATION: Inyo National Forest between U.S. 395 and Rock Creek Canyon; northwest of Bishop and south of Tom's Place.

HIGHLIGHTS: Four-wheeling over an 11,000-foot ridge will reward you with views of glaciated peaks, Rock Creek Canyon and a high basin with a small lake and wind-blown sand dunes. At a vista point at the end is a truly spectacular view across the Owens Valley to the White Mountains.

DIFFICULTY: This is the most challenging route in the book. I rate the road up Sand Canyon moderate, and the road to the top of Wheeler Ridge difficult. I rate the road on the east side of the ridge, to the overlook where I end the drive, moderate. I do not recommend driving beyond the overlook, which would involve a dangerous traverse on a mountainside shelf. You will encounter ledges, very rocky places to maneuver through and steep pitches. Undercarriage scraping is possible. Portions of Sand Canyon Road are rocky with brush.

TIME & DISTANCE: From the start of Sand Canyon Road to Wheeler Ridge Road is about 45 minutes and 7.3 miles one-way. From there, it's about 1.5 hours and 3.4 miles one-way to the overlook, including the spur to the dunes. If you combine this with the remainder of Sand Canyon Road (Tour 24), plan to spend 5-6 hours altogether and add 4 miles. (Sand Canyon Road ends 2 miles beyond the junction with Wheeler Ridge Road.)

MAPS: Inyo National Forest, and the USGS' *Mt. Morgan* 7.5-minute topo map. Sand Canyon Road is on the Inyo NF map (and the Toms Place topo map as well), but Wheeler Ridge Road is not.

INFORMATION: Inyo NF, White Mountain Ranger Station.

GETTING THERE: Take Sand Canyon Road (Tour 24) to Wheeler Ridge Road.

REST STOPS: Have lunch at the overlook.

THE DRIVE: From Sand Canyon Road, follow the road along a meadow and past granite outcrops. Cross a brook, then maneuver between boulders and trees. A mile from the start the trail climbs to a rough, steep and rocky spot. After another mile of uphill four-wheeling you will be on the ridge, looking down at a beautiful basin more than 10,800 feet high, with a small lake. Follow the road down to and across the basin, to a junction. The right branch goes a short distance to sand dunes piled against a mountainside. The left branch edges east above a canyon, then bends south to reach a junction in 0.6 mile. Below to the left is the viewpoint where I end the drive. If you want to explore the mountainside 4WD trail ahead (it ends in about 3 miles at the John Muir Wilderness), hike it. It's not far to another knoll where you can see how the igneous granite is interspersed with chunks of black rock, called inclusions.

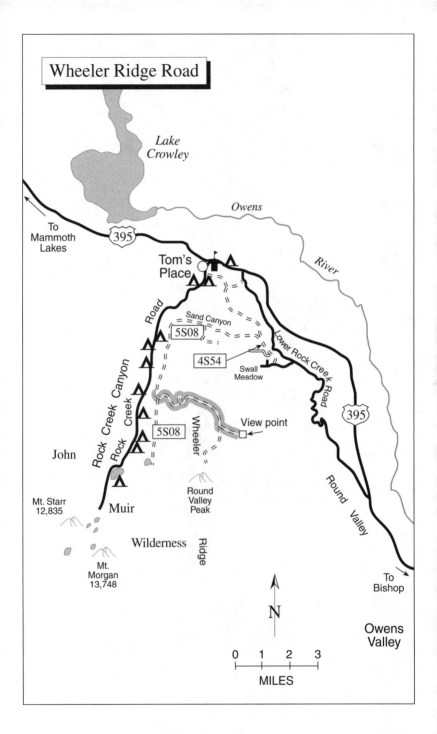

Wheeler Ridge Road

Lake
Crowley

Owens

To
Mammoth
Lakes

395

Tom's
Place

River

Road

Sand Canyon
5S08

4S54

Lower Rock Creek Road

Swall
Meadow

Rock Creek Canyon

Rock Creek

5S08

Wheeler

View point

395

John

Round Valley
Peak

Mt. Starr
12,835

Muir

Round Valley

To
Bishop

Wilderness

Ridge

Mt.
Morgan
13,748

N

Owens
Valley

0   1   2   3
MILES

Wheeler Ridge (Tour 25)

Hot Creek, near Mammoth Lakes.

Laurel Canyon

LOCATION: Inyo National Forest, south of Mammoth Lakes.

HIGHLIGHTS: This is a spectacular and convenient 4WD sojourn from U.S. 395 and Mammoth Lakes, up a glacial moraine and into a breathtaking mountain canyon high on the Sierra's steep eastern escarpment. The views of the Long Valley Caldera (a 75-square mile crater formed by a massive volcanic eruption 700,000 years ago), the Mono Craters (formed 6,000 to 6,500 years ago) and other features of the Sierra's volcanic past are terrific. Aspens along Laurel Creek, which cascades down the bottom of the canyon, make it a good early-autumn drive. It ends at the head of the canyon, near two sparkling lakes (with trout fishing) at the edge of the John Muir Wilderness.

DIFFICULTY: Moderate. A narrow rocky road makes for a slow and bumpy ride. You will encounter switchbacks and one stretch along a talus slope. I've found the road blocked near the end by snow in late July, making for a tricky turnaround.

TIME & DISTANCE: 3 hours; about 9 miles round-trip.

MAPS: Inyo National Forest. *Mammoth Lakes Area Off-Highway Vehicle and Mountain Biking Map*. ACSC's *Eastern Sierra*.

INFORMATION: Inyo National Forest, Mammoth Ranger Station and Visitor Center.

GETTING THERE: A mile southeast of Mammoth Lakes turnoff on U.S. 395, exit west onto Sherwin Creek Road. Drive west for 1.4 miles. Laurel Canyon Road (a.k.a. Laurel Lakes Road), 4S86, is on the left (southwest) side of the road. You can also take Sherwin Creek Road from Old Mammoth Road at the town of Mammoth Lakes. At 4S86 set your odometer at 0.

REST STOPS: There are primitive campsites in the canyon. You will find other camping areas, primitive and developed, in the vicinity of Mammoth Lakes, which has all services.

THE DRIVE: You can see the long, high-walled glacial trough of Laurel Canyon, where the 4WD road climbs up a large moraine, rising from about 7,400 feet to almost 10,000 feet. At mile 2.9 the narrow road crosses a steep talus slope on the canyon's southeastern wall. Beyond is a great view of Laurel Creek cascading down the canyon; behind is Long Valley, a caldera; and to the north are the Mono Craters cones. The road makes a couple of easy switchbacks. Soon you should be able to see whether it's blocked farther up by snow, which tends to linger in the road at about mile 4.4 to 4.5. The road is relatively wide there. If it is blocked, you should be able to park. Just leave room for other visitors. If the road is clear, continue a short way to a wide and flat area that has room to park and turn around. From there the descent to the larger and prettier of the two Laurel Lakes is very rough, with a tight switchback. The road is likely to be obstructed by large rocks. Instead of trying to drive down to the larger lake, I suggest parking and walking. It's about 15-20 minutes down, and 25-30 minutes back up. (Remember, the air is much thinner at this elevation.)

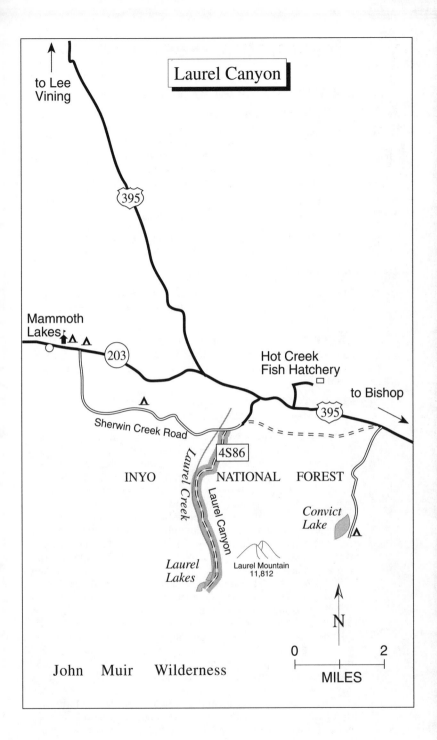

Laurel Canyon

to Lee Vining

395

Mammoth Lakes

203

Hot Creek Fish Hatchery

to Bishop

395

Sherwin Creek Road

4S86

INYO   NATIONAL   FOREST

Laurel Creek

Laurel Canyon

Convict Lake

Laurel Lakes

Laurel Mountain 11,812

N

0   2

MILES

John   Muir   Wilderness

TOUR 27

Mammoth Lakes – Hwy. 120

LOCATION: Inyo National Forest east of Mammoth Lakes.

HIGHLIGHTS: You will cross the wooded, volcanic landscape of the 75-square-mile Long Valley Caldera and the desert in the Sierra's rain shadow. The summits of Lookout Mtn. (8,352 feet) and Bald Mtn. (9,104 feet) provide 360-degree vistas of a vast region, including the escarpment of the eastern Sierra, Mammoth Mtn. (an 11,053-foot dormant volcano) and Mono Basin.

DIFFICULTY: Easy, on high-clearance 2WD roads. Although there are many junctions, the important ones are marked.

TIME & DISTANCE: It's about 4 hours and 53 miles from Mammoth Lakes to Hwy. 120, then 27 miles more to U.S. 395.

MAP: Inyo National Forest.

INFORMATION: Inyo National Forest, Mammoth Ranger Station and Visitor Center, on the north side of Hwy. 203 at Mammoth Lakes.

GETTING THERE: At Mammoth Lakes, turn north off Hwy. 203 west of the Mammoth Ranger Station and Visitor Center, onto road 3S08. Reset your odometer, and drive toward Shady Rest Park.

REST STOPS: There are no services after Mammoth Lakes. Refer to your map for campgrounds.

THE DRIVE: The pavement ends at Shady Rest Park. From there graveled road 3S08 goes through pine forest to U.S. 395. There, you will see two small concrete tunnels that pass beneath the highway. (Check your clearance.) Once through the tunnels the road angles left (north) to road 3S06. Go right (east), and in a short distance turn left (north) onto road 2S02. It will take you 3 miles to the summit of Lookout Mtn. where you can view the volcanic Mammoth region. Mammoth Mtn. dominates a gap in the Sierra that lets moist Pacific air slip through which creates Mammoth's famous snowfall, and the forest that spreads out into the desert from the gap. From here follow 3S06 and then 2S08 north to paved Owens River Road, at Owens River Ranch. Go left (west) there, then turn right (north) into Big Springs CG. Keep to the right, and follow road 2S04 up Alpers Canyon toward Bald Mtn. Lookout, about 10 miles away via road 1S05. 1.4 miles below Bald Mtn., on the left, is smaller road 1S11, which, after you visit the lookout, will take you east for 2.3 miles to Pilot Springs Road (1S04). You'll want to go east there. For now, cross it and take the two-track ahead a short way to a rocky knoll with a great view. Return to 1S04, note your odometer, and continue southeast toward McLaughlin Springs. In 2.7 miles angle left at the bend, and climb to a ridge and a T junction with road 1S17. Note your odometer again, then go right (south). Follow 1S17 over a ridge (chips of obsidian, a black volcanic glass, make the roadbed sparkle here). 8.4 miles from that T turn left (east) onto Taylor Canyon Road (1S17). In 8.7 miles you will be at Hwy. 120. U.S. 395 is left.

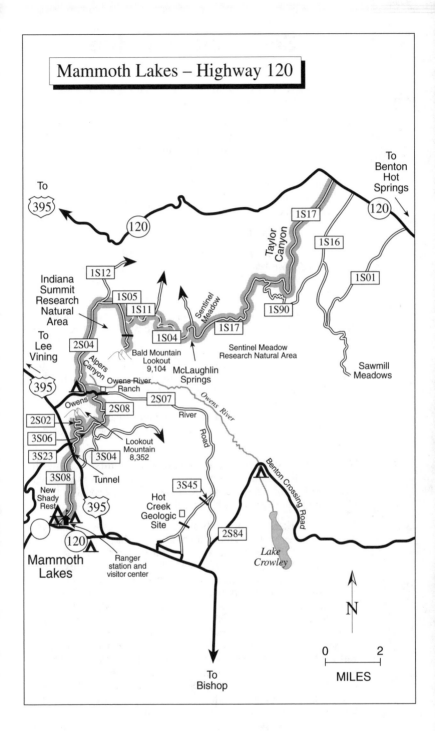

Mammoth Lakes – Highway 120

To 395

120

To Benton Hot Springs

120

1S17

1S16

1S01

Taylor Canyon

1S12

1S05

1S11

1S04

1S17

Sentinel Meadow

1S90

Indiana Summit Research Natural Area

To Lee Vining

395

2S04

Alpers Canyon

Bald Mountain Lookout 9,104

McLaughlin Springs

Sentinel Meadow Research Natural Area

Sawmill Meadows

Owens River Ranch

2S07

2S08

Owens

Owens River

River

Road

2S02

3S06

3S23

Lookout Mountain 8,352

3S04

3S08

Tunnel

395

New Shady Rest

120

Mammoth Lakes

Ranger station and visitor center

3S45

Hot Creek Geologic Site

2S84

Benton Crossing Road

Lake Crowley

To Bishop

N

0   2

MILES

San Joaquin Ridge

LOCATION: West of Mammoth Lakes and north of Hwy. 203 (Minaret Road) at Minaret Summit. Inyo National Forest.

HIGHLIGHTS: This is a short yet terrific drive to over 10,000 feet, where you'll have a head-spinning 360-degree view. The volcanic soil is fragile, so do stay on the road.

DIFFICULTY: Moderate. The road is steep and rutted in places, and winds between trees near the start. I once found the road blocked by a large, shaded snowdrift late in July. Watch for hikers. Parking and turning around space is tight at road's end.

TIME & DISTANCE: 1-1.5 hours; 5 miles round-trip.

MAP: *Mammoth Lakes Area Off-Highway Vehicle and Mountain Biking Map*, available locally. The road is not shown on the Inyo National Forest map, but it's well-established and easy to follow.

INFORMATION: Inyo National Forest, Mammoth Ranger Station and Visitor Center, on the north side of Hwy. 203 at Mammoth Lakes.

GETTING THERE: From Mammoth Lakes, take Hwy. 203 (Minaret Road) toward Minaret Vista and Devils Postpile, driving through the large parking area for Mammoth Mountain Resort. On Minaret Summit, just before the Minaret Vista entrance station, turn right (north) into a dirt area. In a few yards the little San Joaquin 4WD road and bike trail angles left, toward Deadman Pass.

REST STOPS: There are excellent vista points. Mammoth Lakes has all services. You will find a picnic area with parking, tables, toilets and great views at Minaret Vista. Devils Postpile National Monument is nearby as well.

THE DRIVE: Some steep climbing lies ahead: use low range. After 1.5 miles you will reach a shaded spot that can be blocked by snow well into summer. If it is, don't attempt to cross, and don't leave the road to get around it. If clear, the road exits the trees and climbs steeply to a ridge that provides a front-row view of the Minarets, 12 pointy peaks in the Ritter Range of the Sierra Nevada. Named for the towers on mosques, the Minarets are all that remain of a lava flow that predates the Sierra. To the south looms 11,053-foot Mammoth Mountain, a dormant volcano formed some 370,000 years ago that now dominates a forested gap in the Sierra's "rain shadow." Here, moist air slips up the San Joaquin River drainage and through the gap to deliver the heaviest snowfall in the eastern Sierra, an average of 353 inches a year. Gaze east across the volcanic, 75-square-mile Long Valley Caldera, headwaters of the Owens River, to Glass Mountain Ridge, even to the distant White Mountains. About 2.5 miles from Minaret Summit the road ends at a blustery point overlooking Deadman Pass. (My altimeter read about 10,180 feet here.)

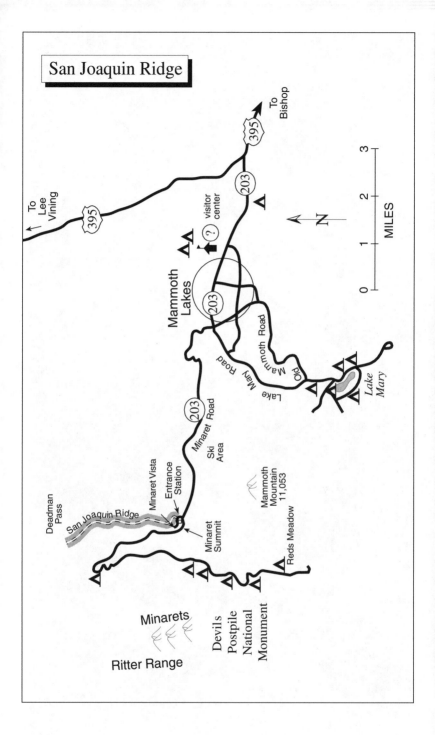

San Joaquin Ridge

Mammoth Mountain, from the San Joaquin Ridge 4WD Road (Tour 28)

Mono County Courthouse, Bridgeport

Horse Meadows Loop

LOCATION: Southwest of Mono Lake and the junction of California Hwy. 120 and U.S. 395, at Lee Vining. Inyo National Forest.

HIGHLIGHTS: This short and convenient tour at the eastern edge of Yosemite National Park takes you past two pretty mountain meadows, Upper and Lower Horse Meadows, on a loop around 8,431-foot Williams Butte. Views reach from the volcanic Mono Craters to the peaks of the Ansel Adams Wilderness and Yosemite. This loop is also a designated and well-marked mountain bike trail, making it easy to follow.

DIFFICULTY: Easy.

TIME & DISTANCE: 45 minutes; 6.5 miles.

MAPS: ACSC's *Eastern Sierra* or its *Guide to Yosemite National Park.* Inyo National Forest's visitor map is useful, but it doesn't show the north-south connecting link that makes this a loop.

INFORMATION: Mono Basin Scenic Area Visitor Center, north of Lee Vining on U.S. 395.

GETTING THERE: 1.2 miles south of the Hwy. 120/U.S. 395 junction, turn west onto Horse Meadows Road (1N16), at the sign for Horse Meadows on the west side of U.S. 395.

REST STOPS: Anyplace you like. Nearby Lee Vining has all services. Refer to your maps for campgrounds in the area.

THE DRIVE: As soon as you pull off the highway and head west on Horse Meadows Road (1N16), you will be looking up at snow-salted peaks as high as 13,053 feet (Mt. Dana). At mile 1.2, just beyond the junction with Aqueduct Road (1N17), you will come to grassy Lower Horse Meadow. In another mile the road enters a narrow granite canyon, and then makes a short but steep climb on a chewed-up stretch. A short distance beyond that, at mile 2.8 or so, the road enters a stand of pines at the edge of a larger meadow, Upper Horse Meadow. (Continuing ahead for 0.7 mile will take you to the Gibbs and Kidney lakes hiking trailhead.) Immediately upon entering the pines, turn left (south), and drive up to the crest of a ridge, where small roads branch left and right. Continue straight ahead (south), and wind down the south side of the ridge, passing through a woodland strewn with large granite boulders. The views of the Sierra's dramatic eastern escarpment will be spectacular as you descend and cross a couple of small streambeds. The route bends to the east, toward U.S. 395, and runs along the base of Williams Butte. Go through another junction with Aqueduct Road, which comes in from the left (north) here, and soon you will be on paved Oil Plant Road, which will bring you to U.S. 395.

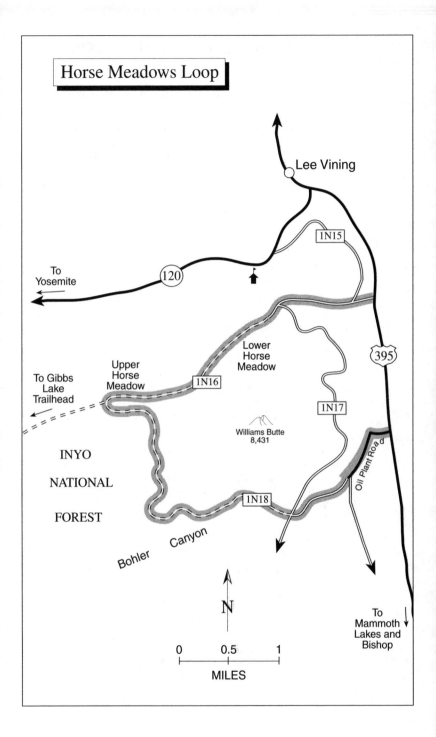

Horse Meadows Loop

Lee Vining

1N15

To Yosemite 120

Upper Horse Meadow

Lower Horse Meadow

1N16

To Gibbs Lake Trailhead

1N17

US 395

Williams Butte 8,431

INYO NATIONAL FOREST

1N18

Oil Plant Road

Bohler Canyon

N

To Mammoth Lakes and Bishop

0   0.5   1
MILES

Copper Mountain Loop

LOCATION: Humboldt-Toiyabe National Forest. Northwest of Mono Lake. West of U.S. 395 and Conway Summit.

HIGHLIGHTS: This loop on Copper Mountain is a convenient side trip from U.S. 395 that provides outstanding vistas, from the eastern Sierra across the volcanic Mono Basin and Bodie Hills to the Great Basin.

DIFFICULTY: Easy.

TIME & DISTANCE: 1 hour; 10.8 miles.

MAP: Toiyabe National Forest, Bridgeport Ranger District.

INFORMATION: Humboldt-Toiyabe National Forest, Bridgeport Ranger District. The Mono Basin Scenic Area Visitor Center, north of Lee Vining on U.S. 395.

GETTING THERE: At Conway Summit, about 12 miles north of Lee Vining on U.S. 395, turn west on Virginia Lakes Road. About 0.4 mile from the highway, turn left (southwest) onto road 180, at a sign for Jordan Basin. Set your odometer at 0.

REST STOPS: Lee Vining has all services. The Mono Basin Scenic Area Visitor Center has restrooms, books, maps, etc. Mono Lake County Park, just off U.S. 395 at the northwest corner of Mono Lake, has picnic areas, bird watching, a playground and restrooms. You'll find camping, food, lodging and other amenities at Virginia Lakes and elsewhere in the area.

THE DRIVE: The road quickly becomes rocky as it meanders up the slopes of Copper Mountain toward Mt. Olsen. Soon you will get panoramic views of Mono Lake (one of the oldest bodies of water in North America), volcanic Mono Craters and other features formed over millions of years by glaciation, volcanic eruptions and faulting. You will also have great views of the long spine of the High Sierra. In 2 miles road 180 reaches road 181 (on the left), which is where you will come out after completing the loop. Continue straight ahead. At mile 3.2 is the other end of road 181, on the left. Take it. It will climb and wind in and out of forest, eventually bringing you to a crest with spectacular view of glacier-carved Lundy Canyon and the peaks of the Hoover Wilderness. At a junction at mile 5.5, go left. In 0.4 mile is another awesome vista point overlooking the Mono Basin. Return to the junction and follow road 181 north. It passes through stands of large aspens, descending until it rejoins road 180. Go right, and retrace your route to Virginia Lakes Road and U.S. 395.

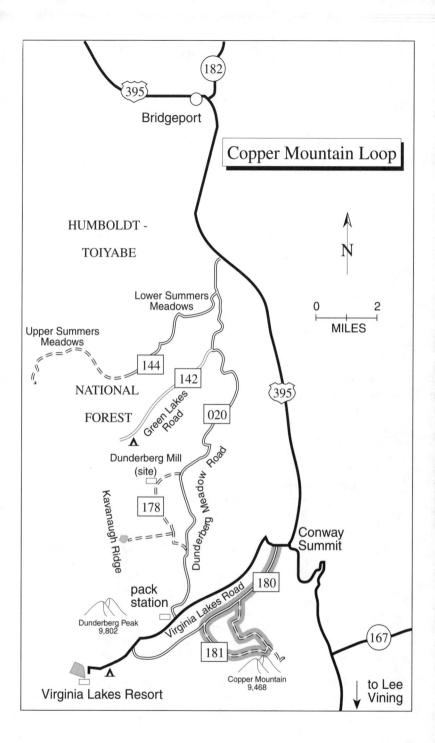

Copper Mountain Loop

182

395

Bridgeport

HUMBOLDT -

TOIYABE

0   2

MILES

Lower Summers
Meadows

Upper Summers
Meadows

144

142

NATIONAL

FOREST

Green Lakes
Road

020

395

Dunderberg Mill
(site)

Dunderberg Meadow Road

Kavanaugh Ridge

178

Conway
Summit

pack
station

Virginia Lakes Road

180

167

Dunderberg Peak
9,802

181

Copper Mountain
9,468

Virginia Lakes Resort

to Lee
Vining

Dunderberg Meadow Road

LOCATION: Humboldt-Toiyabe National Forest, northwest of Mono Lake and just west of the Hoover Wilderness.

HIGHLIGHTS: This is a very scenic drive, with aspen groves and high snowy peaks that make it a great early autumn drive. There's a beautiful unnamed lake (at about 10,250 feet) at the end of a short 4WD spur toward the base of Kavanaugh Ridge. I highly recommend this tour as an alternate route if you're traveling on U.S. 395 and have some extra time. It can be combined with Copper Mountain Loop (Tour 30).

DIFFICULTY: This is an easy and relaxing drive on a maintained road. I rate the spur to the lake moderate. The drive can be taken in either direction, but I think going north, the direction I describe, is the most scenic.

TIME & DISTANCE: 1.5 hours; about 15 miles.

MAPS: Humboldt-Toiyabe National Forest, Bridgeport Ranger District. ACSC's *Eastern Sierra* or its *Guide to Yosemite National Park.*

INFORMATION: Humboldt-Toiyabe National Forest, Bridgeport Ranger District.

GETTING THERE: From 8,138-foot Conway Summit, the highest point on U.S. 395 about 12 miles north of Lee Vining, turn west on Virginia Lakes Road. After about 4.5 miles turn right (north) onto Dunderberg Meadow Road (020), which merges with Green Lakes Road at the northern end leading to U.S. 395. Set your odometer at 0.

REST STOPS: The unnamed lake is a gorgeous place for a break. There are campgrounds at Virginia Lakes, and other amenities at Virginia Lakes Resort.

THE DRIVE: Going north, Dunderberg Meadow Road begins as a good graveled two-lane road. In less than a mile it narrows to a single lane, then winds through pines and across sage- and grass- covered foothills. 1.3 miles from Virginia Lakes Road turn left (west) off Dunderberg Meadow Road onto forest road 178. Follow 178 for 0.3 mile to a Y. Take the left branch. (178 is a rough little 4WD road that continues north through the forest to the site of the old Dunderberg Mill, then reconnects with the main road. There isn't much left of the mill except debris.) This spur is steep at first as it climbs through trees to an open area. In 1.5 miles it will deliver you to a beautiful lake at the base of Kavanaugh Ridge. Back on Dunderberg Meadow Road, you will begin a rapid descent, and eventually see the other end of road 178, which courses up a beautiful valley. Soon you will reach Green Lakes Road (142) and, 3.4 miles farther, U.S. 395.

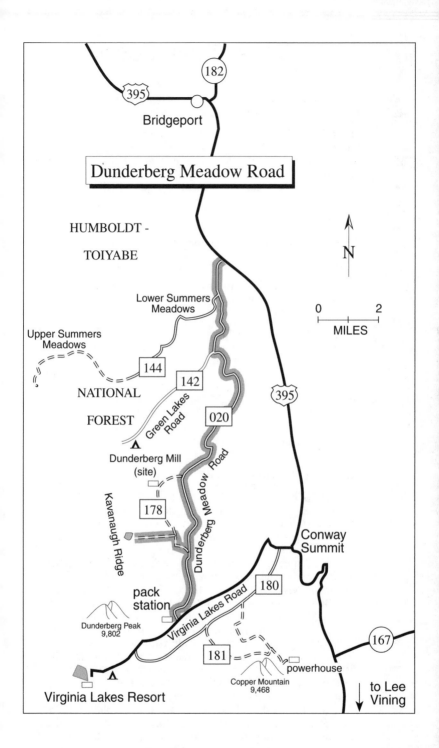

Dunderberg Meadow Road

Ghost Town Loop

LOCATION: Mono County, in the Bodie Hills north of Mono Lake and east of Bridgeport (on U.S. 395).

HIGHLIGHTS: This beautiful high-desert drive takes you into the rolling Bodie Hills, which provide sweeping views of the Sierra Nevada and the Sweetwater mountains to the west. It will take you through a historic mining district that includes the ghost towns of Masonic and, most notably, Bodie, California's best-preserved ghost town.

DIFFICULTY: Easy.

TIME & DISTANCE: 2-3 hours; 32 miles.

MAPS: Toiyabe National Forest, Bridgeport Ranger District.

INFORMATION: Humboldt-Toiyabe National Forest, Bridgeport Ranger District. BLM's Bishop Field Office. Bodie State Historic Park.

GETTING THERE: In Bridgeport, take state Hwy. 182 north for 3.8 miles from the junction with U.S. 395. Turn east onto Masonic Road (046). Set your odometer at 0. A remote but more interesting option is to take Calif. Hwy. 182/Nev. 338 north for 15 miles from Bridgeport, then turn east onto Sweetwater Road (028). In 1.8 miles turn south onto the northern leg of Masonic Road (046), and follow it for 6.7 miles into the hills to the site of Masonic, and continue the tour from there. This option, however, bypasses Chemung Mine and the spur to the summit of Masonic Mountain.

REST STOPS: There are toilets and a picnic area at Bodie.

THE DRIVE: After 5 miles the graded road reaches the ruins of Chemung Mine, on the right, as you circle around 9,217-foot Masonic Mountain. This scenic stretch provides views of a range of features, particularly the Sierra and Sweetwater mountains, as it climbs to a saddle. At 7.7 miles from the highway you will reach a 1.2-mile spur to the right that will take you up to an electronic site atop Masonic Mountain, where there's an outstanding 360-degree vista. From there the road descends to the junction with Bodie-Masonic Road (169), at the Upper Town section of bygone Masonic, a town spawned by a gold discovery in 1902. Masonic grew into three sections: Upper, Middle and Lower Town. The gold in these hills didn't follow any pattern, and finally ran out. Scavengers have hauled off most, but not all, of the town's remains over the years. Go left (north) on Masonic Road (046) through a canyon, and you will soon reach the sites of Middle Masonic and Lower Town. There will be a few ruins alongside the road, and old mines are still visible on the hillsides. Return to the junction at Upper Town, and follow road 169 east up a long draw, then south for almost 14 miles. You will eventually round a turn, and find yourself looking down on old Bodie, once a raucous and short-lived gold-mining town that grew to 10,000 souls during its heyday in 1879-1881. Today, it is maintained for posterity in a state of "arrested decay."

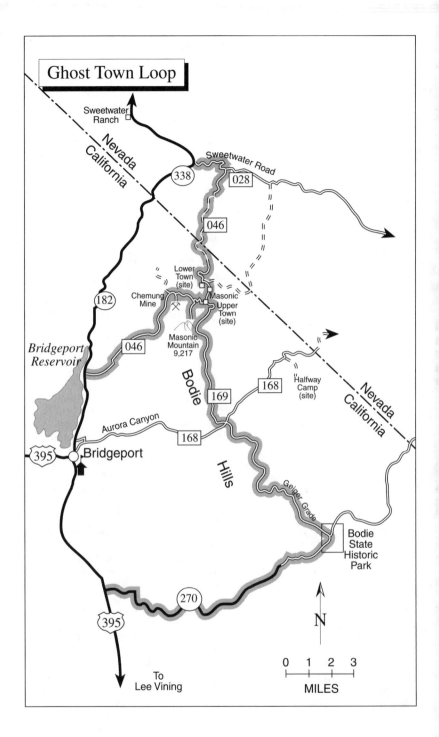

Ghost Town Loop

Sweetwater Ranch

Nevada
California

Sweetwater Road

338
028
046

Lower Town (site)
Chemung Mine
Masonic Upper Town (site)

182

046

Bridgeport Reservoir

Masonic Mountain 9,217

Bodie

169
168

Halfway Camp (site)

Nevada
California

Aurora Canyon

168

395
Bridgeport

Hills

Geiger Grade

Bodie State Historic Park

270

395

N

0 1 2 3
MILES

To Lee Vining

Boulder Flat

LOCATION: In the Sweetwater Mountains. Humboldt-Toiyabe National Forest, 11 miles due north of Bridgeport (on U.S. 395). West of Nevada Hwy. 338 and the California/ Nevada line.

HIGHLIGHTS: The high-elevation vistas are magnificent in this old gold- and silver-mining district, with spectacular vistas and peaks that exceed 11,000 feet.

DIFFICULTY: Easy to moderate.

TIME & DISTANCE: 2 hours and 18.2 miles round-trip to Boulder Flat, excluding the time you spend there. The additional routes described will add another 1-2 hours and 5.4 miles.

MAP: Toiyabe National Forest, Bridgeport Ranger District.

INFORMATION: Toiyabe NF, Bridgeport Ranger District.

GETTING THERE: From Bridgeport, go north on Hwy. 182, which becomes Nevada Hwy. 338 at the state line. About 18.6 miles from the U.S. 395/Hwy. 182 junction, turn left (west) at Sweetwater Ranch onto Atchison Road (191). Zero the odometer.

REST STOPS: There are primitive campsites at Boulder Flat.

THE DRIVE: Keep to the left at the ranch, and drive slowly through it. At a fork at mile 1.1 go through a gate, then turn left (south) onto road 198 where road 191 continues toward the mountains. After several creek crossings there's a fork at mile 2.1, immediately after crossing a cattle guard (where the road crosses from Nevada into California). Road 198 goes right (west). Take it, and begin the rocky climb. At mile 4.9 make a hard right between pines, then climb to a flat at mile 6.2, where Star City once stood. Angle right, cross the flat, then go left at the wooden post. The mountainside road will fork in 0.2 mile; keep left. A short distance farther, the route (road 198) bends right (a two-track goes straight). The road becomes even rockier as it ascends toward a yellow-orange mountain. At mile 8.1 you will emerge into pretty Boulder Flat, a basin and mining camp site at the base of 11,664-foot Wheeler Peak. Two log buildings of uncertain age and a number of foundations can be seen. The elevation is about 10,300 feet. The road bends right (north) across Boulder Flat, passing among pines. It goes to a vista point in a mile, and ends at the inactive Frederick Mine just beyond that. Back at the cabins, where you first entered Boulder Flat, go south through the trees, past another old log structure to a pond and a flat area. This is the vicinity of the bygone mining camp of Belfort. The road descends via switchbacks to a gap where it follows Fryingpan Creek upstream to Long Meadow. There, go left across the creek. The climb here (on road 098) isn't difficult. At the top is a view of the Sierra from about 10,700 feet. Turn around here.

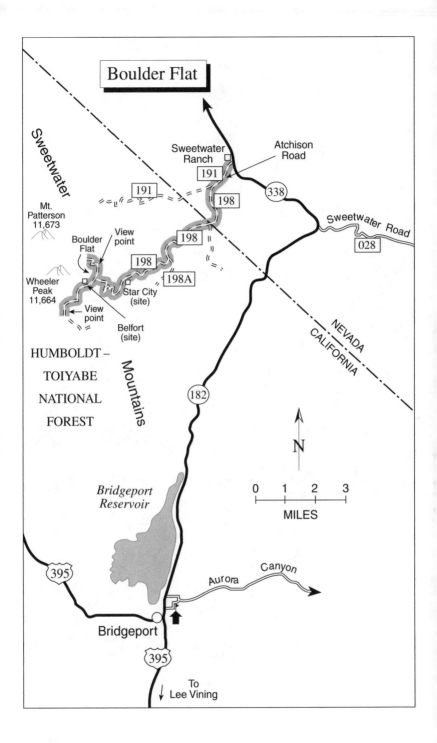

Boulder Flat

Sweetwater

Mt. Patterson 11,673

Boulder Flat

View point

Wheeler Peak 11,664

Star City (site)

View point

Belfort (site)

HUMBOLDT – TOIYABE NATIONAL FOREST

Mountains

Sweetwater Ranch

Atchison Road

191

191

198

338

Sweetwater Road

028

198

198

198A

182

NEVADA

CALIFORNIA

Bridgeport Reservoir

N

0   1   2   3
MILES

395

Aurora Canyon

Bridgeport

395

To ↓ Lee Vining

Boulder Flat (Tour 33)

California/Nevada stateline, Ghost Town Loop (Tour 32)

Burcham Flat Road

LOCATION: Southwest of the Nevada line, in the Sweetwater Mountains just east of U.S 395 and the Sierra. Humboldt-Toiyabe National Forest. This high north-south road parallels the Walker River and U.S. 395, between Walker and Fales Hot Springs.

HIGHLIGHTS: In January 1844 explorer Capt. John C. Fremont, guide Kit Carson and a small band of half-starved men passed this way looking for the fabled Ventura River, which they thought would give them easy passage through the Sierra, to the west. They ended up forcing their way through the mountains in winter instead. You will enjoy outstanding mountain scenery on this alternative to U.S. 395, which signs spell as BIRCHAM but which maps show spelled as Burcham.

DIFFICULTY: Easy. This is a maintained 2WD road, but the loose soil and gravel can make using high-range 4WD advisable if you start at the north end.

TIME & DISTANCE: 45 minutes; 15 miles.

MAP: Toiyabe National Forest, Bridgeport Ranger District.

INFORMATION: Humboldt-Toiyabe National Forest, Bridgeport Ranger District.

GETTING THERE: This drive, which connects to U.S. 395 at both ends, can be driven north or south. The scenery is outstanding in both directions. **To go south** (the way I describe)**:** At the east end of Walker, on U.S. 395, turn north onto paved Eastside Road. Almost 1.2 miles from the highway, turn right (east) onto paved Camp Antelope Road. Go 0.2 mile, then veer right (southeast) onto unpaved Burcham Flat Road (031). **To go north:** Take U.S. 395 north from Bridgeport for 14.6 miles. Turn right (north) onto Burcham (the sign spells it Bircham) Flat Road. Set your odometer at 0.

REST STOPS: Anyplace that appeals to you. Bridgeport is a pretty little town with all services.

THE DRIVE: Going south from Walker, Burcham Flat Road climbs fairly steeply through semi-arid canyons, taking you high above the canyon of the Walker River and U.S. 395. Soon the road angles into the mountains. After a few miles you're getting outstanding views, especially as the road takes you over a hill. You suddenly have the Sierra looming up ahead and to the west. Be sure to stop now and then and take in the equally dramatic alpine scenery behind you. At mile 11.6 the road crosses a summit, at about 8,000 feet, and soon takes you past the turnoff to Lobdell Lake and Jackass Flat (Tour 35). Then comes the long, rapid descent on a manicured segment of road through Burcham Flat to U.S. 395. Watch your speed as you descend, because it's easy to lose control on gravel.

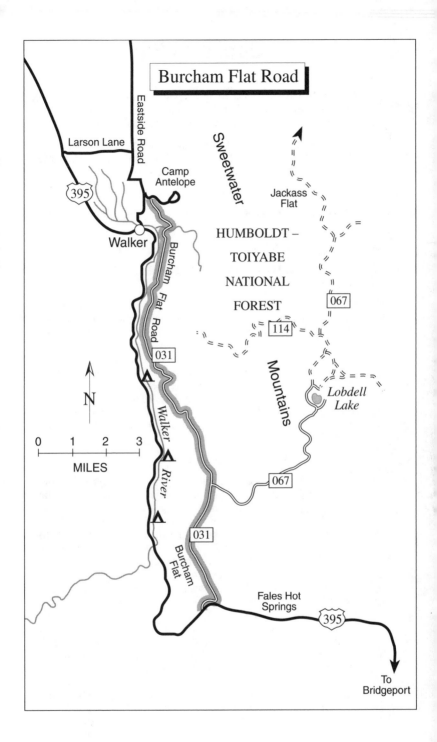

Burcham Flat Road

Eastside Road

Larson Lane

395

Camp Antelope

Sweetwater

Jackass Flat

HUMBOLDT –
TOIYABE
NATIONAL
FOREST

067

114

Walker

Burcham Flat Road

031

Walker River

Mountains

Lobdell Lake

067

N

0   1   2   3
MILES

031

Burcham Flat

Fales Hot Springs

395

To Bridgeport

Jackass Flat

LOCATION: Just west of the Nevada-California state line in Mono County; east of Walker and northwest of Bridgeport in the Sweetwater Mountains. Humboldt-Toiyabe National Forest.

HIGHLIGHTS: You will have spectacular views of the Sierra Nevada from a ridgeline drive high in the Sweetwater Mountains, a beautiful range east of the Sierra.

DIFFICULTY: Easy to moderate.

TIME & DISTANCE: 2.5 hours; 24.4 miles from U.S. 395 to Risue Road.

MAP: Toiyabe National Forest, Bridgeport Ranger District.

INFORMATION: Humboldt-Toiyabe National Forest, Bridgeport Ranger District.

GETTING THERE: This north-south route can be taken in either direction. The scenery is great either way. **To go north** (the way I describe it): From U.S. 395 about 14.6 miles northwest of Bridgeport, turn north onto Burcham (also spelled Bircham) Flat Road (031). 4.3 miles north of U.S. 395, turn east onto road 067 and follow it to Lobdell Lake (about 6.2 miles from Burcham Flat Road). At a Y at the southeast corner of the lake, set your odometer at 0 and go left. **To go south:** Follow the directions to Risue Road (Tour 36). Take Risue Road east for 5.2 miles, then turn right (south) onto road 195 and follow it south to road 067.

REST STOPS: Anyplace that's appealing.

THE DRIVE: Going north, road 067, the road you will follow for most this tour, runs along the west side of Lobdell Lake, then north of it. About 2.3 miles north of the Y at the southeast corner of the lake is another, smaller Y. Go left (west). About 0.2 mile farther, at another small Y, 067 angles right (north), up a hill, and climbs to a high, rocky and exposed ridge. Here you will have terrific vistas of the Sierra and the Sweetwater Mountains. The latter include the three "sisters"—East Sister (10,402 feet), Middle Sister (10,859 feet) and South Sister (11,339 feet), as well as Mount Patterson (11,673 feet) and Wheeler Peak (11,664 feet). The two-track road of loose rock follows the ridge north. By mile 5.7 you will descend steeply to a 4-way junction. Follow the road that goes north from the junction, along the west-facing mountain slope. By about mile 7.4 you will be crossing broad Jackass Flat, where you may welcome the softer roadbed after so much rocky ridge-running. At mile 9.4 the road passes Jackass Spring, marked by a corral. 0.4 mile after that is another junction. Take the left (north) branch, road 195. This easy road will cross the Nevada/California line three times, bringing you to Risue Road, on the Nevada side, by mile 14. Go left (west), and drive 5.2 miles to Eastside Road, then south into California and the town of Walker, on U.S. 395. Or go right and take the scenic Risue Road tour.

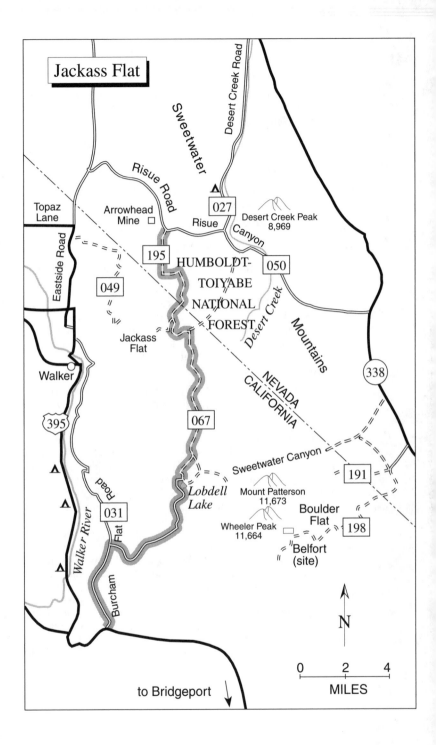

Jackass Flat

Sweetwater

Desert Creek Road

Risue Road

Topaz Lane

Arrowhead Mine □

△ 027

Risue Canyon

Desert Creek Peak 8,969

195

HUMBOLDT-TOIYABE

050

Eastside Road

049

NATIONAL

Desert Creek

Mountains

Jackass Flat

FOREST

NEVADA
CALIFORNIA

Walker

395

067

338

Sweetwater Canyon

191

Lobdell Lake

Mount Patterson 11,673

Boulder Flat

Walker River

Road

Flat

031

Wheeler Peak 11,664

198

Belfort (site)

△

△

Burcham

△

N

0   2   4
MILES

to Bridgeport ↓

Risue Road

LOCATION: In Nevada, just east of the state line in the Sweetwater Mountains of Humboldt-Toiyabe National Forest; northeast of Walker (on U.S. 395).

HIGHLIGHTS: This tour of the semi-arid desert that lies in the Sierra's rain shadow takes you along deep and very scenic Risue Canyon. It connects with the Jackass Flat drive (Tour 35).

DIFFICULTY: Easy, although the western end of this maintained road can be very slick when wet.

TIME & DISTANCE: 1 hour; about 16.5 miles.

MAP: Toiyabe National Forest, Bridgeport Ranger District.

INFORMATION: Toiyabe National Forest, Bridgeport Ranger District.

GETTING THERE: From Walker, on U.S. 395: Follow Eastside Road north for 8.4 miles. Turn right (east) at the well-marked turnoff for Risue Road (050). **From U.S. 395 south of Topaz Lake:** Take Topaz Lane east to Eastside Road (3.5 miles). Take Eastside Road north for about 1.8 miles to the junction with Risue Road. Set your odometer to 0.

REST STOPS: Stop along Desert Creek on the canyon floor, after you pass Desert Creek Road. You will see some primitive campsites.

THE DRIVE: This fun and very scenic cruise will take you from about 5,460 feet elevation to about 7,300 feet on a good dirt-and-gravel road. About 1.2 miles from Eastside Road you will enter Risue Canyon, as you follow what likely will be a dry wash. By mile 2.8 it becomes a one-lane mountain road. Note the old Arrowhead Mine on the right at mile 4. At mile 5.2 is the road (195) to Jackass Flat. As you continue to climb, by mile 6 you will cross a summit, at about 7,300 feet. As the road descends it will pass through much heavier vegetation, then follow along the wall of a deep, rocky and wooded canyon. At mile 7.9 is a turnout with a great view. A short distance farther is the turn north for Desert Creek Road (027). Stay on Risue Road, and the canyon floor will soon become something of an oasis with some appealing, though undeveloped, campsites. After you climb out of the canyon, the undulating road will deliver you to Nevada Hwy. 338.

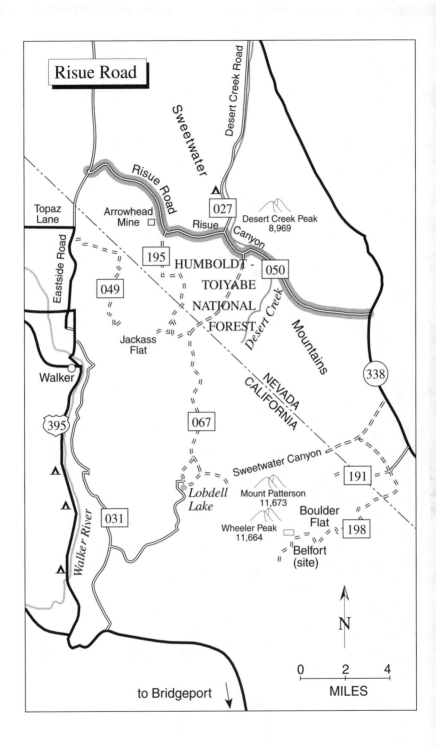

Risue Road

Topaz
Lane

Eastside Road

Arrowhead
Mine

Sweetwater

Risue Road

Desert Creek Road

027

Risue Canyon

Desert Creek Peak
8,969

195

HUMBOLDT -

050

049

TOIYABE

NATIONAL

Desert Creek

Mountains

FOREST

Jackass
Flat

NEVADA

CALIFORNIA

338

Walker

395

067

Sweetwater Canyon

191

Lobdell
Lake

Mount Patterson
11,673

031

Wheeler Peak
11,664

Boulder
Flat

198

Belfort
(site)

Walker River

N

0   2   4
MILES

to Bridgeport

Slickrock Trail

LOCATION: South of Hwy. 4 at Lake Alpine. Stanislaus National Forest, at the west edge of the Carson-Iceberg Wilderness.

HIGHLIGHTS: This isn't Moab, Utah's, famous mountain-biking trail. Instead, it's a short and beautiful 4WD trail to a granite expanse where you can picnic in the shade beside lovely Silver Creek. Experienced four-wheelers can continue beyond where I stop, on a challenging 4x4 trail to Utica Reservoir.

DIFFICULTY: The narrow route is rocky in places, making high clearance and skid plates mandatory. I rate it moderately difficult as far as I take you. Beyond that, the Forest Service gives the 4x4 trail to Utica Reservoir a rating of very difficult. I've not made the trek, but I'm told that stock SUVs do make it through.

TIME & DISTANCE: From Hwy. 4 it is 1.5 hours, depending on how much time you spend at Silver Creek; 3.6 miles round-trip.

MAP: Stanislaus National Forest.

INFORMATION: Stanislaus National Forest, Calaveras Ranger District. Alpine Guard Station, near Bear Valley.

GETTING THERE: Take Hwy. 4 to the west end of Lake Alpine. Set the odometer at 0, then turn south onto the paved road to the Lake Alpine campground. Just beyond the campground the road forks. The left branch is blocked, so you have to go right, on road 7N01. The pavement ends 0.1 mile from the highway.

REST STOPS: Silver Creek. There are developed campgrounds in the vicinity of Lake Alpine; refer to your map. Primitive camping along this route is allowed after the first 0.7 mile.

THE DRIVE: Watch for potholes as you wind through pine forest, on what is still an easily traveled road along the lake's southwestern shore. At mile 0.5 from the highway, angle right (a private driveway is on the left), and the road will diminish to a narrow, single-lane track through the forest. You will find it necessary to go slow as you maneuver between trees and over the roadbed rocks, so this might be a good time to shift into low-range for better low-speed control. At about mile 1.5 the trail, and I do call it a trail, brings you to gorgeous Silver Creek. There is a substantial rock ledge to get over here. From now on you will see many places where the stream cascades through the surface granite, but none is more idyllic than the oasis you will reach by mile 1.8. You can park here, and let the kids wade in the stream and play among the pines for a truly memorable outing. If you want to consider continuing on to Utica Reservoir, walk a short distance farther down the trail to inspect a rocky granite crack that you'll have to crawl through.

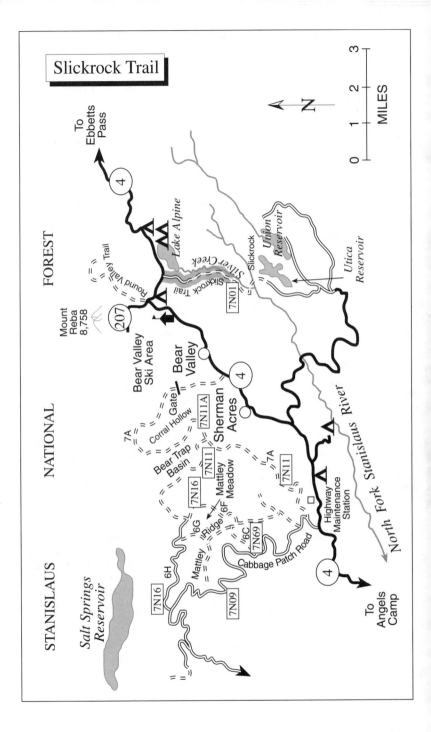

Slickrock Trail

Bear Trap-Corral Hollow

LOCATION: Stanislaus National Forest. North of Hwy. 4 and west of Bear Valley and Lake Alpine.

HIGHLIGHTS: This drive winds through forest and meadows thick with mule's ear, a tall, leafy plant that flowers in late July. The drive mixes tight maneuvering between obstacles with easy cruising and culminates in spectacular views of the Mokelumne Wilderness and the central Sierra from a 6,500-foot-high ridge between the drainages of the Mokelumne and Stanislaus rivers, and the meadows at Corral Hollow and Bear Trap Basin. Jelmini Basin has huge aspens.

DIFFICULTY: The eastern leg, route 7A from Hwy. 4 near Bear Valley to Bear Trap Basin is moderate to difficult. The Corral Hollow trail (7N11 & 7N11A) between Cabbage Patch Road (7N09) and Bear Trap Basin, is easy. Be prepared to maneuver between trees and rocks, and to remove deadfall from the roadway.

TIME & DISTANCE: 3 hours; 14 miles.

MAPS: Stanislaus National Forest. Also get a copy of the Calaveras Ranger District's off-highway vehicle route map.

INFORMATION: Stanislaus NF, Calaveras Ranger District.

GETTING THERE: This loop can be taken in either direction. To evaluate the rougher segment early on, begin on route 7A at Hwy. 4, about 0.6 mile west of Bear Valley. Look for a small sign with a 4WD symbol on the north side of the highway, and a CORRAL HOLLOW OHV ROUTE sign. Reset your odometer there. To go in the opposite direction: 6.8 miles southwest of Bear Valley turn north from Hwy. 4 onto Cabbage Patch Road (7N09). In 0.9 mile turn right at the sign for road 7N11 to Corral Hollow.

REST STOPS: Old Bear Trap cabin, in Bear Trap Basin, is a pleasant place. You'll also find the only toilet on the route there.

THE DRIVE: Route 7A is a slow, narrow, rutted, rocky but pretty forest trail that passes or crosses a number of meadows. There is a steep and loose uphill section at mile 1.8, but at mile 2.3 you will be amply rewarded for your effort when you reach a ridge overlooking the canyon of the North Fork of the Mokelumne River, and the Mokelumne Wilderness. (You're also next to Bear Valley's ski runs.) The route angles left (west) here, climbing high along the ridge to a spectacular viewpoint at mile 3. Then the road descends southward through the meadow of Corral Hollow. At mile 3.8 is a chewed-up spot, but it shouldn't be a problem. By mile 5.2 you will enter a picturesque meadow, Bear Trap Basin, where you will see Bear Trap Cabin, an old cowboy cabin now owned by the Forest Service. The road south is much better. It climbs out of the basin and makes a long, scenic descent to the southwest via roads 7N11A & 7N11. At mile 1.8 from Bear Trap Basin, 4WD road 7N11 spurs to the right (northwest), to Jelmini Basin, where the aspens are remarkably large. Continuing south, you will reach Cabbage Patch Road (7N09) in 4.7 miles. Go left there, and soon you will be at Hwy. 4.

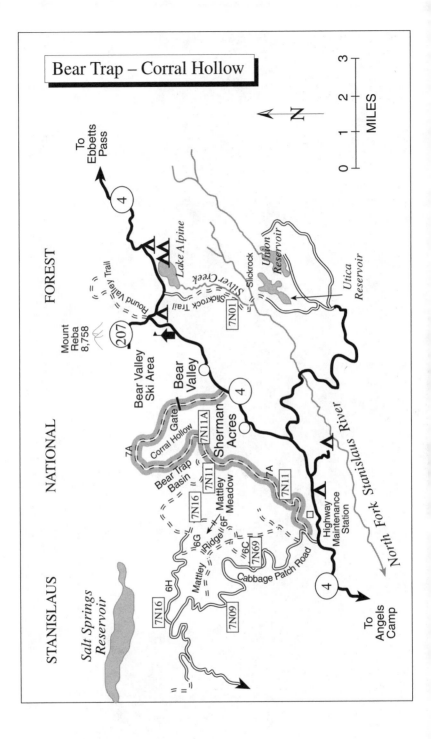

Bear Trap – Corral Hollow

Bear Trap Basin and Bear Trap Cabin (Tour 38)

4WD trail sign

Round Valley Trail

LOCATION: North of Hwy. 4 at Lake Alpine. Stanislaus National Forest.

HIGHLIGHTS: This is a convenient, short but exhilarating 4WD road that climbs steeply to a summit about 8,842 feet high, with spectacular vistas across the Sierra and into the canyons and valleys of the Mokelumne Wilderness. It ends at the wilderness boundary, at the Lake Valley trailhead of the Tahoe-Yosemite Trail.

DIFFICULTY: Moderate. The road is steep, rocky and chewed up in places.

TIME & DISTANCE: 45 minutes; 5.3 miles round-trip.

MAP: Stanislaus National Forest, and the Calaveras Ranger District's off-highway vehicle trail brochure.

INFORMATION: Stanislaus National Forest, Calaveras Ranger District. The Alpine Guard Station, at Bear Valley.

GETTING THERE: 0.1 mile west of Silvertip Campground, just west of Lake Alpine, turn north from Hwy. 4 onto Hwy. 207 toward the Bear Valley ski area. 0.1 mile from Hwy. 4, look for a dirt road on the right (east) side of the road marked by a 4WD symbol (like the one pictured on p. 115) and an orange arrow. That is the route.

REST STOPS: The summit is a great place to spend time. You will find many amenities, including campgrounds, at Lake Alpine.

THE DRIVE: This road used to be the Mt. Reba Trail, because it used to go up to a lookout on the top of nearby Mt. Reba. Now, though, the road ends at a summit about a mile from Mt. Reba, an easy hike. (But Mt. Reba is lower, at 8,758 feet.) It winds steeply through forest and across open hillsides above the east end of Round Valley, providing magnificent high-elevation views of the glacial valleys, lakes, canyons, and granite domes and spires of the High Sierra. At mile 2.2 from Hwy. 207 is a fork; keep left. You will reach the summit 2.7 miles from Hwy. 207.

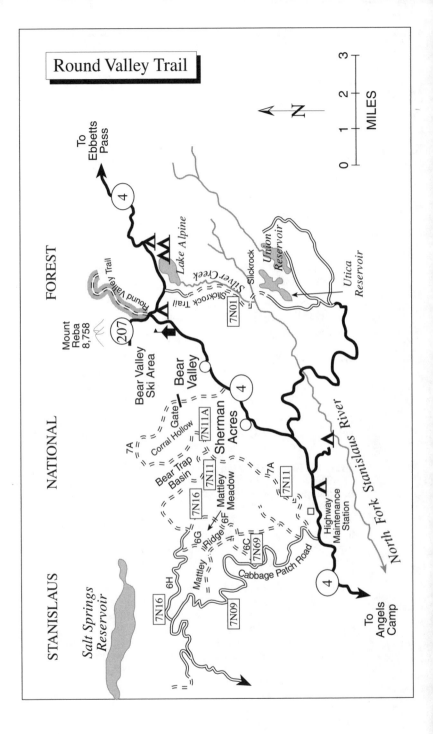

Round Valley Trail

Mattley Ridge Loop

LOCATION: Stanislaus National Forest. North of Hwy. 4 and west of Bear Valley and Lake Alpine.

HIGHLIGHTS: This rather unique Sierra drive mixes moderate four-wheeling with easy cruising through a range of landscapes, from forest to Mattley Meadow, where the trail passes through areas thick with a large leafy plant, commonly called mule's ear, which flowers in late July. It also provides outstanding high-elevation vistas across the canyons, valleys and peaks of the rugged Mokelumne Wilderness.

DIFFICULTY: Moderate to difficult, with some maneuvering between narrowly spaced trees and rocks. Be prepared to either remove or maneuver around deadfall in the roadway.

TIME & DISTANCE: 1.5 hours; 8.6 miles. There are variations and other worthwhile routes to explore in the area.

MAPS: Stanislaus National Forest. Also get a copy of the Calaveras Ranger District's off-highway vehicle route map.

INFORMATION: Stanislaus NF, Calaveras Ranger District.

GETTING THERE: 6.8 miles southwest of Bear Valley turn north from Hwy. 4 onto Cabbage Patch Road (7N09). Take Cabbage Patch Road north 3.9 miles, then turn right (northeast) onto road 7N69 (OHV trail 6C). Reset your odometer.

REST STOPS: Anywhere you find appealing. You'll find food and fuel at Bear Valley. There are many developed campgrounds in the area; refer to your map.

THE DRIVE: Like many roads and trails in this area, road 7N69 is a designated off-highway vehicle route with an additional numeric designation (6C) on the Calaveras District's OHV route map. Watch for signs with those designations. You will also see yellow arrows denoting OHV routes. This one climbs up to Mattley Ridge. At mile 1, on the ridge, you will reach a junction; OHV route 6A is to the left and right. This is the Mattley Ridge Loop, a designated OHV route that you will follow but leave toward the end. Go right. In a half-mile take a narrow, rudimentary 4WD road (6F) that angles to the left and descends down the north side of the ridge to sprawling and lush Mattley Meadow. The road follows the perimeter of the meadow, then enters it at mile 2.6 amid stands of unusually large aspens. Here the narrow road passes through a meadow thick with leafy mule's ear, providing a unique Sierra driving experience. At mile 3.9 is a much better road, 7N16 (6H). Just before you reach it, you will have to make a very tight maneuver between a boulder and a tree. Go left (west) on 7N16, and in 1.5 miles OHV route 6G branches to the left to climb back up to Mattley Ridge via one particularly nasty spot, and complete the loop where you began. I recommend continuing west on 7N16, which provides great views of the canyon of the North Fork of the Mokelumne River and the Mokelumne Wilderness before taking you back to Cabbage Patch Road in 4.7 miles.

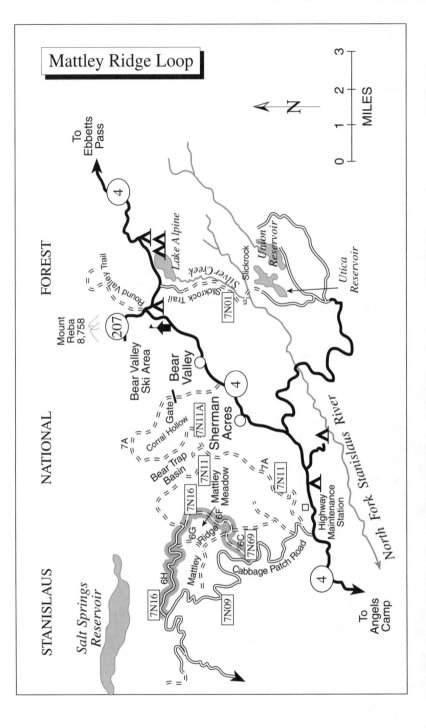

Mattley Ridge Loop

Leviathan Peak Loop

LOCATION: Just north of Hwy. 89 at Monitor Pass. Humboldt-Toiyabe National Forest.

HIGHLIGHTS: You will find outstanding views from the crest of the Sierra, especially if you take the short side trip to the nearby summit of Leviathan Peak (8,963 feet).

DIFFICULTY: Easy.

TIME & DISTANCE: 1.5 hours; 5.3 miles. Can be taken in either direction.

GETTING THERE: From the junction of Hwys. 89 and 4 south of Markleeville, drive east on Hwy. 89 for 7.6 miles to Monitor Pass. Or from U.S. 395 south of Topaz Lake, take Hwy. 89 west for 8 miles to Monitor Pass. In a large meadow just west of the roadside historical marker on the pass, turn north from Hwy. 89 onto road 083, a two-track to the right of two ponds. Drive toward a saddle with a rocky peak on the left and a rock outcrop on the right. Reset the odometer to 0 at the highway.

MAP: Toiyabe National Forest, Carson Ranger District.

INFORMATION: Humboldt-Toiyabe National Forest, Carson Ranger District.

REST STOPS: Anyplace that appeals to you.

THE DRIVE: You're going to circle around the base of Leviathan Peak, which offers a fantastic 360-degree panorama from the summit. At about mile 0.6 there's a spur to the left, which will go a short distance to a ridge with views of the valley to the west. Soon the main road veers east, at nearly 8,400 feet, giving you fine vistas of Nevada's desert ranges. At 1.8 miles from the highway you will pass through a large aspen grove, which promises a spectacular display of color in early autumn. At mile 3.4 is a rocky downhill pitch. At mile 3.6 you will come to a fork; go straight. At mile 3.8 the road takes you past Big Spring, to your left, as you head south toward the highway. A quarter-mile farther take a track to the left. It will take you a short distance to Indian Springs Road (085; Tour 42). Go right when you reach it, toward the highway, just half a mile away. To go up Leviathan Peak, from Hwy. 89 just east of the Monitor Pass historical marker take the short drive up Leviathan Lookout Road (057). Part-way up you will have to park at a locked gate, then walk about a quarter-mile to the lookout tower on the summit. The incredible vista there makes it worth every step.

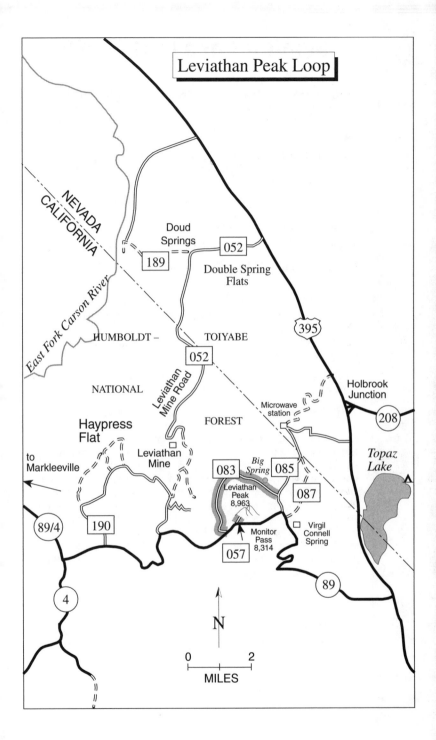

Leviathan Peak Loop

Monitor Pass to U.S. 395

LOCATION: This tour follows Indian Springs Road (a.k.a. the 085 road) down from Monitor Pass on Hwy. 89 to U.S. 395 in Nevada, just north of Topaz Lake. Humboldt-Toiyabe National Forest.

HIGHLIGHTS: You will make an exhilarating 2,600-foot descent from Monitor Pass to U.S. 395, on a mountainside road with an outstanding view east into the Great Basin.

DIFFICULTY: Easy, but there are long drop-offs.

TIME & DISTANCE: An hour; 7 miles.

MAP: Toiyabe National Forest, Carson Ranger District.

INFORMATION: Humboldt-Toiyabe National Forest, Carson Ranger District.

GETTING THERE: From the junction of Hwys. 89/4 south of Markleeville: Take Hwy. 89 east almost 10 miles to Monitor Pass. From U.S. 395: Take Hwy. 89 west a little more than 7 miles to Monitor Pass. Turn north onto Indian Springs Road (085). Set the odometer at 0.

REST STOPS: It's a short drive, so just stop at appropriate places to enjoy the view.

THE DRIVE: From Hwy. 89, Indian Springs Road is a good dirt and gravel backway. You will pass 8,963-foot Leviathan Peak, to your left (you can drive to within a short distance of the top, where the view from a fire lookout is even more incredible). At mile 2.7, as you pass through rolling hills of sagebrush and grass, the road crosses the Nevada line. You'll see an electronics site ahead; drive toward it, and turn right when you get there. Now you will have a great view of the Carson Valley, far below. At mile 3.5 there's a fork to the left; go straight, staying on the gravel road. The view is absolutely magnificent at this point, as you wind down the mountainside on what becomes a good single-lane road. Eventually the road levels out and comes out at U.S. 395 north of Topaz Lake.

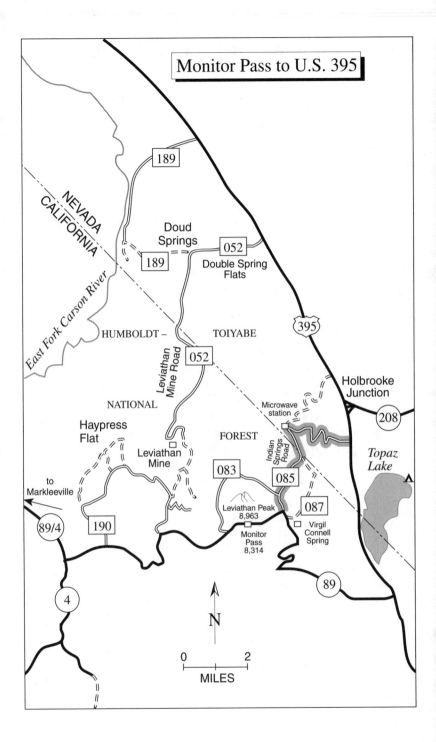

Monitor Pass to U.S. 395

Haypress Flat Loop

LOCATION: Alpine County, north of Hwy. 89. East of Markleeville. Humboldt-Toiyabe National Forest.

HIGHLIGHTS: Road 190, a.k.a. Morningstar Road, and the side road to Haypress Flat will take you through a beautiful corner of the Sierra where the superlative scenery includes the High Sierra, meadows and canyons. Stands of aspen make it a fine late-summer or early-autumn drive. There is quite a network of optional, and sometimes rough, 4WD spurs to explore as well. The mines in this old mining district add interest, but require caution. This tour can be linked with Leviathan Mine Road (Tour 44).

DIFFICULTY: Easy overall, but spurs can be much more difficult. Old mine sites are dangerous.

TIME & DISTANCE: 1.5 hours; 9.4 miles.

MAP: Toiyabe National Forest, Carson Ranger District.

INFORMATION: Carson Ranger District. Markleeville Guard Station, in Markleeville.

GETTING THERE: About 1.7 miles east of the intersection of Hwys. 89 and 4 south of Markleeville, turn north from Hwy. 89 onto road 190, Morningstar Road. Set your odometer at 0.

REST STOPS: No place formal, but you will see some primitive campsites and scenic places to stop.

THE DRIVE: At the turnoff from Hwy. 4, where you will see large tailings piles, is the site of the vanished town of Monitor (later called Loope), a center for silver, copper and some gold mining from the late 1850s to the late 1890s. The road climbs steeply but easily up Loope Canyon. At mile 1 you're at the top of the canyon, where road 190 angles right. At mile 1.5 road 190 will make a hard right bend, and you will see a pullout and a good primitive campsite on the left with a great view down into Mogul Canyon. At mile 1.8 road 190B branches left (north). (You can continue on road 190 for a shorter but still very worthwhile version of this tour.) 190B will take you on a scenic loop of about 3.2 miles, through pretty Haypress Flat and then south to rejoin road 190 only 1.5 miles northeast of this point. Or, instead of taking 190B south to rejoin 190, go a bit farther north and east across Haypress Flat, and take road 056 south to rejoin road 190. Back on 190, you will descend through conifers and aspen stands, get a peek at Leviathan Mine and come out on Leviathan Mine Road (052). You can go left (north), past Leviathan Mine to U.S. 395. Or to complete this tour, go right (south) to reach Hwy. 89 in 1.5 miles.

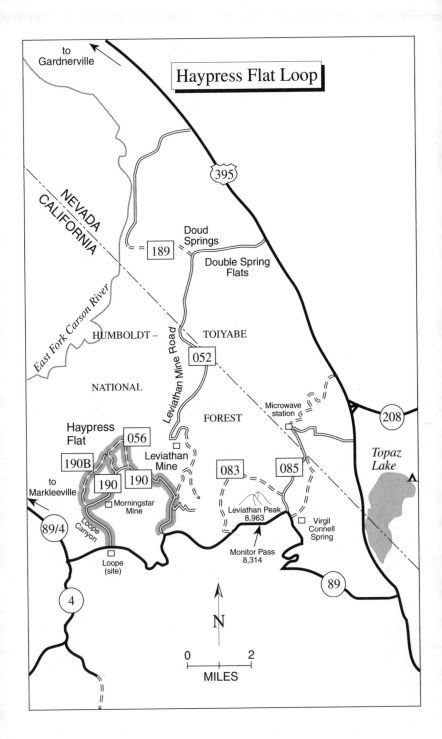

Haypress Flat Loop

to Gardnerville

NEVADA
CALIFORNIA

395

Doud Springs

189

Double Spring Flats

East Fork Carson River

HUMBOLDT –

TOIYABE

052

NATIONAL

Leviathan Mine Road

Microwave station

208

FOREST

Haypress Flat

056

190B

190   190

083   085

Topaz Lake

Leviathan Mine

to Markleeville

89/4

Morningstar Mine

Leviathan Peak 8,963

Virgil Connell Spring

Loope Canyon

Loope (site)

Monitor Pass 8,314

4

89

N

0   2
MILES

Leviathan Mine Road

LOCATION: On the California-Nevada line, between California Hwy. 89 west of Monitor Pass and U.S. 395. Humboldt-Toiyabe National Forest.

HIGHLIGHTS: The inactive Leviathan open-pit sulfur mine, proposed in 1999 for mitigation under the federal Superfund program, and the acid mine drainage that has sterilized streams and threatened the East Fork of the Carson River are a shocking anomaly in an otherwise beautiful area. This drive will take you through forests, canyons and high-desert mountains, and past the mine itself. It can be linked with Haypress Flat (Tour 43).

DIFFICULTY: Easy, on a maintained dirt-and-gravel road. Be careful on the blind curves.

TIME & DISTANCE: 1 hour; 15 miles.

MAP: Toiyabe National Forest, Carson Ranger District.

INFORMATION: Toiyabe National Forest, Carson Ranger District. Markleeville Guard Station.

GETTING THERE: From Hwy. 89 (the way I describe it): From the junction of Hwys. 89/4 south of Markleeville, take Hwy. 89 east for 4.7 miles. Turn left (north) onto Leviathan Mine Road (052). Or take Hwy. 89 west from U.S. 395 for about 12 miles, then turn right (west) onto Leviathan Mine Road. **From U.S. 395:** Leviathan Mine Road (052) is 9.9 miles south of the traffic light at Pinenut Road, at the south end of Gardnerville, Nev. Set your odometer to 0.

REST STOPS: You will see a number of places to stop, particularly where the road is high above the mine.

THE DRIVE: Leviathan Mine Road is a good dirt-and-gravel county road in the high country of the Sierra's eastern slope. At mile 1.5 is the left (west) turn for Morningstar Road (190) and Haypress Flat. Almost a mile farther, angle right where a sign warns that the road is not suited for passenger cars. From here you will come upon places that provide a bird's-eye view of Leviathan Mine, an inactive sulfur mine dating back to 1863, when extraction of copper sulfate was used for processing silver ore in Nevada's Comstock Lode. The off-and-on mining that occurred there afterwards ended in 1962, but the environmental devastation has continued. About 22 million tons of overburden and waste rock were dumped into and along the channels of Leviathan and Aspen creeks when the mine was active. Water seepage into and through the pit, and huge tailings piles create acid mine drainage that runs into Leviathan Creek. Today, Leviathan and Bryant creeks are devoid of aquatic life, and fish kills have occurred in the East Fork of the Carson River, 10 miles downstream. Beyond the mine you will drive along beautiful Leviathan Canyon, cross the Nevada line and then head east across Double Spring Flat to U.S. 395 south of Gardnerville.

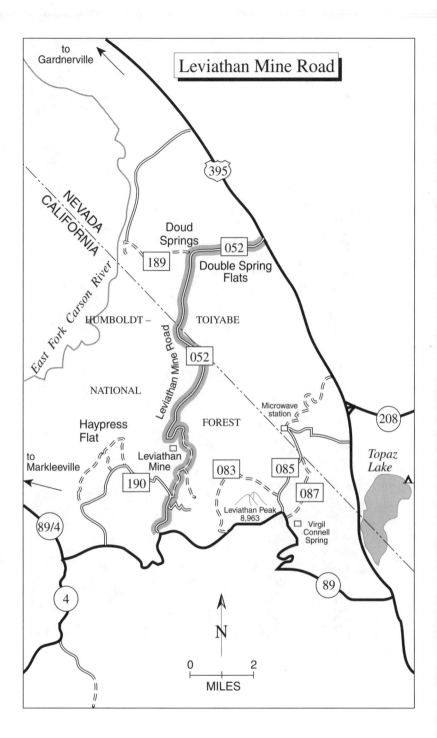

Leviathan Mine Road

to
Gardnerville

395

NEVADA
CALIFORNIA

Doud
Springs

052

189

Double Spring
Flats

East Fork Carson River

HUMBOLDT –

TOIYABE

052

NATIONAL

Leviathan Mine Road

Microwave
station

208

Haypress
Flat

FOREST

to
Markleeville

Leviathan
Mine

083

085

190

087

Topaz
Lake

Leviathan Peak
8,963

Virgil
Connell
Spring

89/4

4

89

N

0   2

MILES

Leviathan Mine, California (Tour 44)

Lake Tahoe from Genoa Peak (Tour 46)

TOUR
45

Blue Lakes & Indian Valley

LOCATION: Eldorado National Forest, south of Hwy. 88 and Carson Pass, at the edge of the Mokelumne Wilderness.

HIGHLIGHTS: There are many beautiful lakes and meadows, as well as vistas of the Mokelumne Wilderness. There are opportunities for hiking, camping, fishing and mountain biking.

DIFFICULTY: Forestdale Road (a.k.a. Forestdale Creek Road) and Blue Lakes Road are easy. Blue Lakes Road is paved for 6 miles south of Hwy. 88, then it's maintained gravel for the next 6 miles or so to Lower Blue Lake (this segment is expected to be paved eventually). About 3 miles south of Red Lake, Forestdale Road becomes a narrow shelf road that can be blocked by slow-melting snow well into summer. The roads in the Little Indian Valley and Indian Valley areas are easy to moderate.

TIME & DISTANCE: 1.5-2 hours and 20 miles for the loop around Blue Lakes alone. The segment to Indian Valley adds 8-10 miles and another 1-1.5 hours or so.

MAP: Eldorado National Forest.

INFORMATION: Eldorado NF, Amador Ranger District.

GETTING THERE: This loop can be taken in either direction, beginning or ending at Hwy. 88. I describe it starting at the eastern end of Red Lake, just east of Carson Pass: Take the Red Lake turnoff south onto Forestdale Creek Road (013), then the left fork through a large green gate. Set your odometer at 0 there.

REST STOPS: Lost Lakes and Forestdale Divide are pretty. There are developed campgrounds at Upper and Lower Blue Lakes, and at Hope Valley near Hwy. 88. You'll find primitive camping areas in the Indian Valley area as well (use sites).

THE DRIVE: At 1.5 miles Forestdale Road crosses a bridge over Forestdale Creek. You'll see signs for Lost Lakes and Upper Blue Lake. A short distance farther is a fork; keep right. The road will climb, becoming a single lane at mile 1.9. By mile 3 you're at a point where I've found the road blocked by snow as late as August. Just beyond there is Forestdale Divide, where the road and the Pacific Crest Trail intersect in a sub-alpine setting at about 8,800 feet. Descend from there toward Upper and Lower Blue Lakes, but take the spur to pretty Lost Lakes. (There is an optional spur later on, via road 9N01 to Twin and Meadow lakes, that is worth exploring as well.) There are fairly steep stretches beyond the Lost Lakes turnoff as you drive through forest to Upper Blue Lake. At the southern tip of Lower Blue Lake, turn east and then north on Blue Lakes Road (015), a busy road in summer that follows the Carson River's West Fork to reach Hwy. 88 in about 12 miles (the latter half of the road is paved). After a mile turn right (southeast) onto Sunset Lake Road (097), and follow it to Indian Valley and Little Indian Valley, where there is a network of small roads (with stream crossings) to several lakes. After that, continue to the highway on Blue Lakes Road.

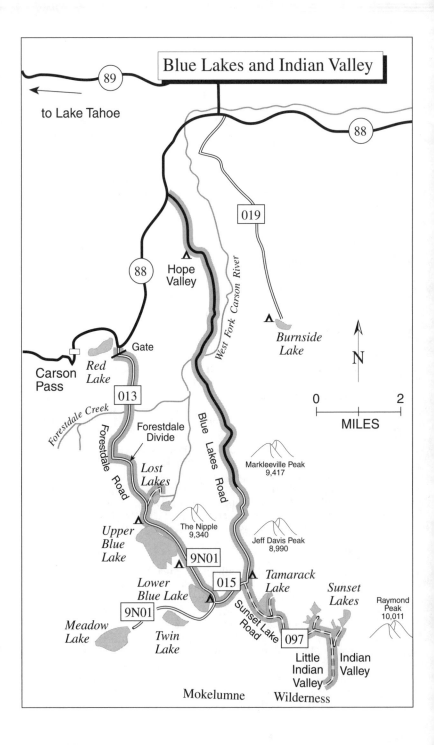

Blue Lakes and Indian Valley

Genoa Peak Road

LOCATION: This tour is on the Nevada side of the Lake Tahoe Basin. It extends between U.S. 50 at the north end (just south of Spooner Junction) and Nevada Hwy. 207 at Daggett Pass at the south end. The road follows the crest of the Carson Range, at the east edge of the Lake Tahoe Basin Management Unit.

HIGHLIGHTS: This high (over 8,000 feet much of the way) mountain road provides great views of the Lake Tahoe Basin, especially from the 9,150-foot summit of Genoa Peak. Along the northern segment, Logan House Road, a side route just west of Genoa Peak Road, is a pretty alternative to Genoa Peak Road.

DIFFICULTY: Easy.

TIME & DISTANCE: 2 hours; 10.2 miles for Genoa Peak Road, including the Genoa Peak spur (one mile round-trip). Logan House Road is 6.5 miles, but omits a portion of Genoa Peak Road.

MAP: Lake Tahoe Basin Management Unit.

INFORMATION: LTBMU. Lake Tahoe Visitors Center.

GETTING THERE: You can take this north-south drive in either direction. **To go north** (the way I describe it): From the junction of U.S. 50 and Nevada Hwy. 207, on the lake's south-eastern shore, take Hwy. 207 east for 2.8 miles, up the Kingsbury Grade toward Daggett Pass. Turn left (north) onto North Benjamin Drive, which becomes Andria Drive. About 1.7 miles from Hwy. 207 is the non-motorized Tahoe Rim Trail. Set your odometer at 0 here. Genoa Peak Road (14N32) is directly ahead. **To go south:** From Glenbrook, take U.S. 50 east toward Spooner Junction, at Ponderosa Ranch Road. Just before the junction, turn right (east) off the highway and drive around behind the Nevada Department of Transportation's Spooner maintenance station, where Genoa Peak Road begins. Logan House Road (14N33) is 1.5 miles from U.S. 50, on the right.

REST STOPS: Genoa Peak.

THE DRIVE: At the south end, Genoa Peak Road used to be an eroding maze of dirt tracks. In addition to erosion control efforts, the Forest Service has obliterated the confusing spurs, and now the route is easy to follow. About 1.3 miles north of the Tahoe Rim trailhead, the road crosses a small basin. Go straight, over a hump. At about mile 3.5 is the left (west) turn for Logan House Road (14N33 on the signposts; 14N24 on the map). Look for a white DESIGNATED ROUTE marker. It's a pleasant drive through aspen stands, meadows and conifer forest strewn with granite. Despite logged areas, some consider it a prettier alternative to the bypassed section of Genoa Peak Road. (It rejoins Genoa Peak Road in 6.5 miles.) About 0.8 mile north of this southern junction with Logan House Road is the right (east) turn to Genoa Peak, where you'll find a 360-degree panorama of the Lake Tahoe Basin and, to the east, the Carson Valley. (One option is to go up to Genoa Peak, then backtrack to Logan House Road.) After a steady, easy descent Genoa Peak Road will deliver you to U.S. 50 at the Nevada DOT station.

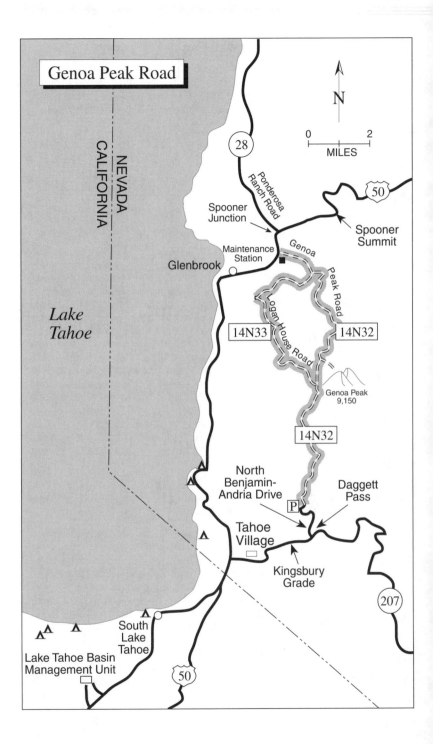

Genoa Peak Road

NEVADA
CALIFORNIA

28

Ponderosa Ranch Road

50

Spooner Junction

Spooner Summit

Maintenance Station

Glenbrook

Genoa Peak Road

Lake Tahoe

14N33

Logan House Road

14N32

Genoa Peak 9,150

14N32

North Benjamin-Andria Drive

P

Daggett Pass

Tahoe Village

Kingsbury Grade

207

South Lake Tahoe

50

Lake Tahoe Basin Management Unit

0   2
MILES

N

Barker Pass Loop

LOCATION: In the Forest Service's Lake Tahoe Basin Management Unit. West of Lake Tahoe, Hwy. 89 and McKinney Bay. Links Tahoma and Idlewild.

HIGHLIGHTS: Pretty lakes and streams, waterfowl, mountains.

DIFFICULTY: Easy to moderate, with road conditions ranging from asphalt to graded dirt, loose rock and large mud holes.

TIME & DISTANCE: About 2.5 hours; 19 miles.

MAP: Lake Tahoe Basin Management Unit.

INFORMATION: LTBMU. Lake Tahoe Visitor's Center.

GETTING THERE: You can take this loop from two points on Hwy. 89 on Lake Tahoe's west shore. **From Tahoma** (the way I take you, so you can appraise the roughest section early): Turn southwest off Hwy. 89 onto paved McKinney-Rubicon Springs Road and follow the signs for Miller Lake. Cross Evergreen Way, and follow the OHV (off-highway vehicle) signs to the McKinney-Rubicon OHV staging area. The pavement ends there. Continue on road 3013. **From Idlewild:** Turn west from Hwy. 89 onto paved Blackwood Canyon/Barker Pass Road (road 3). In 2.2 miles, where the road bends left to cross Blackwood Creek, continue ahead on graveled road 15N38 through the Blackwood Canyon OHV staging area. Follow 15N38 (moderate) along Middle Fork Blackwood Creek to Barker Pass Road (3.8 miles). Go right (west) there for 1.3 miles, then turn left (south) onto road 3013.

REST STOPS: There are toilets at the OHV staging areas, primitive campsites at Miller, Richardson and Bear lakes, and a developed campground at Kaspian.

THE DRIVE: Beyond the asphalt at the McKinney-Rubicon OHV staging area, the road (3013) is rocky, loose and steep. Along the way you may see some 4-wheelers heading to or returning from the famously difficult Rubicon 4WD Trail. About 2 miles from the OHV area is McKinney Lake, where you will encounter a series of large and deep mud holes to get around. Then the road will pass Lily Lake and, beyond that, Miller Lake, where you might see waterfowl. (There's more solitude at Richardson Lake, an easy mile up a left turn just beyond Miller Lake.) 1.2 miles from Miller Lake, across from a parking area and near a bridge, is the turnoff for the Rubicon Trail. Follow the main road through the gate, and climb north past pretty Bear Lake. About 5 miles from Bear Lake is a T-intersection. Go right to reach Barker Pass in about 1.3 miles. It's about a half-mile from the summit to pavement and another 6.9 miles to the highway. For more fun and scenery, turn into and drive through the Pacific Crest Trail parking area and take the 4WD road (15N38) along Middle Fork Blackwood Creek. 15N38 connects to Blackwood Canyon Road 2.2 miles west of Hwy. 89.

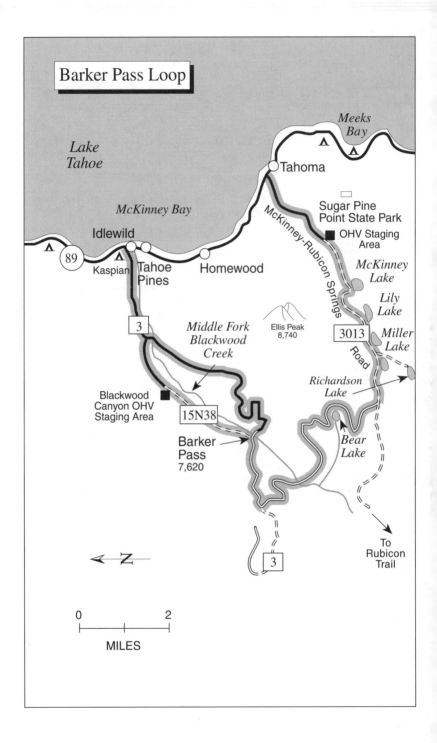

Barker Pass Loop

Lake Tahoe

Meeks Bay

McKinney Bay

Tahoma

Sugar Pine Point State Park

OHV Staging Area

Idlewild

(89)

Kaspian

Tahoe Pines

Homewood

McKinney-Rubicon Springs

McKinney Lake

Lily Lake

3

Ellis Peak 8,740

Middle Fork Blackwood Creek

3013 Road

Miller Lake

Richardson Lake

Blackwood Canyon OHV Staging Area

15N38

Barker Pass 7,620

Bear Lake

To Rubicon Trail

3

← N

0   2
MILES

Mt. Watson

LOCATION: North of Tahoe City, between Hwys. 89 and 267. In the Forest Service's Lake Tahoe Basin Management Unit.

HIGHLIGHTS: The 8,424-foot summit of Mt. Watson provides a terrific view of Lake Tahoe, with more great views of the Sierra on the way down.

DIFFICULTY: Easy, on former logging roads.

TIME & DISTANCE: 1.5-2 hours; 16.4 miles round-trip from Brockway Summit, on Hwy. 267.

MAP: Lake Tahoe Basin Management Unit.

INFORMATION: Lake Tahoe Basin Management Unit. Lake Tahoe Visitors Center.

GETTING THERE: From Lake Tahoe's north shore (the way I take you): Take Hwy. 267 (North Shore Boulevard) about 3.2 miles northwest to Brockway Summit. **From Truckee:** Take Hwy. 267 (Brockway Road) southeast to Brockway Summit. At Brockway Summit turn west onto Mt. Watson Road (73). Set your odometer to 0. You will see on the map that road 06 (easy) also will get you from Truckee to Mt. Watson (12 miles).

REST STOPS: Watson Lake, and the summit of Mt. Watson.

THE DRIVE: For the first 4 miles you will be on a graveled forest road. Then the gravel ends, and the roadbed becomes more rocky. At mile 5.9 you will see road 16N73C on the left. It goes 0.7 miles to Watson Lake. From this turnoff, it's about 0.7 miles farther to road 73M, a fairly steep two-track that angles sharply to the left. This is the road to the summit of Mt. Watson. It's about 1.6 miles from here to the summit, along a mountainside shelf, and the view from the top is absolutely magnificent. The view is great going down as well, but of course the driver will miss it because he or she is paying close attention to the road.

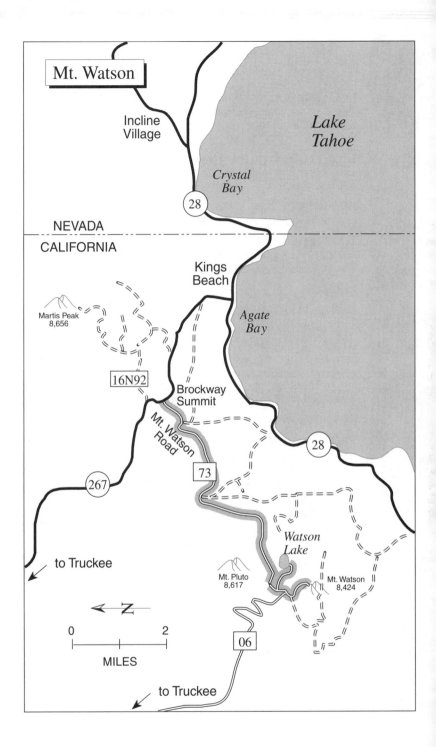

Martis Peak

LOCATION: At the northern edge of the Forest Service's Lake Tahoe Basin Management Unit, 4 miles due north of Kings Beach on Lake Tahoe's north shore, and about 1.5 miles west of the California-Nevada line.

HIGHLIGHTS: Stunning views of the Tahoe Basin and surrounding region from the historic Martis Peak fire lookout, built in 1914.

DIFFICULTY: Easy to moderate. Steep and a bit rocky toward the end.

TIME & DISTANCE: About 1.5 hours; 8 miles round-trip from Hwy. 267 (a.k.a. Brockway Road from Truckee; North Shore Boulevard from Kings Beach).

MAP: Lake Tahoe Basin Management Unit.

INFORMATION: Lake Tahoe Basin Management Unit. Lake Tahoe Visitors Center.

GETTING THERE: Take Hwy. 267 about 3.2 miles northwest from King's Beach over Brockway Summit, or about 8.5 miles southeast from Truckee toward Brockway Summit. About 0.4 mile north of the summit, take the first eastbound road (Martis Peak Road, 16N92), along Martis Creek. Set your odometer to 0.

REST STOPS: The summit of Martis Peak.

THE DRIVE: After turning up Martis Creek, drive 1.9 miles to an intersection, then continue ahead on road 16N92. You might see something like "Martis Pk" spray-painted on a tree trunk to indicate the way. At mile 2.6 is another intersection. Go straight. At almost mile 3.3 is a fork. A rough trail, No. 92B, goes straight, but you don't want that. Go left (the road may not have a sign). About a half-mile farther the road will become steep and rocky. Vistas will appear, and soon you will see the old fire lookout. Drive up to it and park. Climb up to the lookout and take in an amazing sight. You're at 8,656 feet on the lookout. Lake Tahoe is at 6,229 feet.

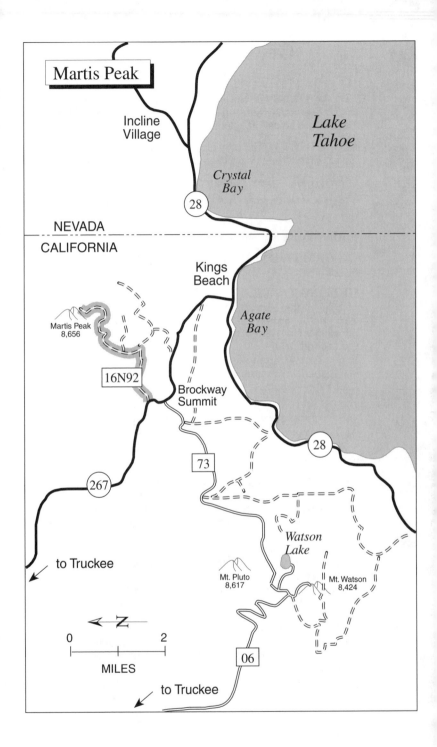

Crystal Peak Loop

LOCATION: Humboldt-Toiyabe National Forest, just west of the California/Nevada line about 5 miles northwest of Verdi, Nev., which is just off I-80 about 10 miles west of Reno.

HIGHLIGHTS: This convenient and highly scenic tour provides vistas across Dog Valley to Reno and into the Great Basin.

DIFFICULTY: Easy, but the roadbed is rocky in places.

TIME & DISTANCE: 1.5 hours; 20 miles starting and ending in Verdi.

MAP: Toiyabe National Forest, Carson Ranger District.

INFORMATION: Humboldt-Toiyabe NF, Carson Ranger District.

GETTING THERE: In Verdi, zero the odometer at the junction of U.S. 40 (the main street) and Bridge Street, then take Bridge Street northwest toward Dog Valley/Henness Pass Road. Go past the elementary school and cross two bridges. Immediately after the second bridge turn right, onto Dog Valley/Henness Pass Road (Tour 4), and follow it through a residential area. At mile 0.9 you will cross from Nevada into California. Continue toward Dog Valley. The pavement ends at mile 1.5, in the national forest.

REST STOPS: Crystal Peak Park along the Truckee River, at the west end of Verdi, is a lovely place to have a picnic. Dog Valley Campground has shade, tables and pit toilets, but no potable water.

THE DRIVE: Road 002, Dog Valley/Henness Pass Road, passes through a gate and climbs gradually up a ravine lined with pines, some of them charred by wildfires. At mile 3.9 is a fork. Take the right branch (Long Valley Road; still 002), and soon you will begin descending into the bowl of Dog Valley. The road passes the Dog Valley Guard Station at mile 5.4. At mile 5.8 turn left onto road 038, which soon becomes crystalline-white in color. You will reach another junction at mile 6.3, where the spur (038) to Dog Valley Campground branches right. Take road 073 directly ahead (there may be a small sign for the Crystal Peak Loop). It will become a narrow shelf that takes you up the west wall of Dog Valley just below 8,103-foot Crystal Peak, eventually switchbacking higher and providing fabulous views east across the valley to Reno and into the desert beyond. (Across the valley looms Peavine Peak. If you look at your map, you will see that you can drive across the valley and make a great loop around the base of the peak, and even up to it.) After following the shelf north, you will switchback down to reconnect with road 038. Go left, again passing Dog Valley Campground, and retrace your route to Verdi.

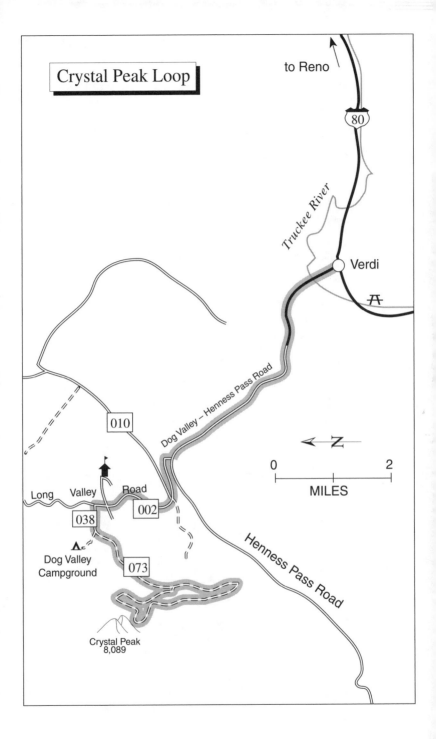

Crystal Peak Loop

to Reno

80

Truckee River

Verdi

Dog Valley – Henness Pass Road

010

Long Valley Road

002

038

073

Dog Valley Campground

Crystal Peak
8,089

Henness Pass Road

0   2
MILES

APPENDIX

Information Sources

4X4NOW.com &
4X4BOOKS.com
Books, maps, advice, articles, etc.

Automobile Club of
Southern California
3333 Fairview Road
Costa Mesa, CA 92626
(714) 427-5950
www.aaa-calif.com

Bureau of Land Management
www.ca.blm.gov/caso/

Bakersfield Field Office
3801 Pegasus Drive
Bakersfield, CA 93308-6837
(661) 391-6000
www.ca.blm.gov/bakersfield

Bishop Field Office
785 N. Main St., Suite E
Bishop, CA 93514
(760) 872-4881
www.ca.blm.gov/bishop

California State Office
2800 Cottage Way
Room W-1834
Sacramento, CA 95825-1886
(916) 978-4400
www.ca.blm.gov/caso/

Jawbone Station
28111 Jawbone Canyon Road
P.O. Box D
Cantil, CA 93519
(760) 373-1165
e-mail: jawbone@ccis.com

Bodie State Historic Park
P.O. Box 515
Bridgeport, CA 93517
(760) 647-6445
http://ceres.ca.gov/sierradsp/bodie.
html

California Association
of 4WD Clubs
8120 36th Avenue
Sacramento, CA 95824-2304
(916) 381-8300
www.cal4wheel.com

California Campground
Reservation System
(877) 444-6777

California State
Automobile Assoc.
150 Van Ness Avenue
San Francisco, CA 94102
(415) 565-2012
www.csaa.com

Eldorado National Forest
Information Center
3070 Camino Heights Drive
Camino, CA 95709
(530) 644-6048
www.r5.fs.fed.us/eldorado/html/
infoctr.htm

Amador Ranger District
26820 Silver Drive
Pioneer, CA 95666
(209) 295-4251

**Eastern Sierra
Interpretive Assoc.**
190 E. Yaney St.
Bishop, CA 93514
(760) 873-2411
www.r5.fs.fed.us/inyo/esia/index.
htm

**Humboldt-Toiyabe
National Forest**
Supervisor's Office
1200 Franklin Way
Sparks, NV 89431
www.fs.fed.us/htnf

> **Bridgeport Ranger District**
> HCR 1 Box 1000
> Bridgeport, CA 93517
> (760) 932-7070
> www.fs.fed.us/htnf/bptodo.htm

> **Carson Ranger District**
> 1536 South Carson St.
> Carson City, NV 89701
> (775) 882-2766
> www.fs.fed.us/htnf/cartodo.htm

Inyo National Forest
873 N. Main St.
Bishop, CA 93514
(760) 873-2400
www.r5.fs.fed.us/inyo/index.htm

> **Ancient Bristlecone Pine
> Visitor Center**
> White Mountains' Schulman
> Grove
> (760) 873-2500 (recorded info.)
> Open only in summer
> www.r5.fs.fed.us/inyo/vvc/bcp/
> index.htm

Inyo National Forest (cont.)
> **Eastern Sierra Interagency
> Visitor Center–Lone Pine**
> P.O. Box R
> Lone Pine, CA 93545-2017
> (760) 876-6222
> Intersection of Hwys. 395 & 136
> www.r5.fs.fed.us/inyo/vvc/
> mtwhtny/index.htm

> **Mammoth Lakes Ranger
> Station & Visitor Center**
> P.O. Box 148
> Mammoth Lakes, CA 93546
> (760) 924-5500
> www.r5.fs.fed.us/inyo/vvc/
> mammoth/index.htm

> **Mono Basin Scenic Area
> Visitor Center**
> U.S. 395 just north of
> Lee Vining
> P.O. Box 429
> Lee Vining, CA 93541
> (760) 647-3044
> www.r5.fs.fed.us/inyo/vvc/
> mono/index.htm

> **Mt. Whitney Ranger Station**
> P.O. Box 8
> Lone Pine, CA 93545
> Hwy. 395 at south end of
> Lone Pine
> (760) 876-6200

> **White Mountain
> Ranger Station**
> 798 N. Main St.
> Bishop, CA 93514
> (760) 873-2500

Lake Tahoe Basin Management Unit
U.S. Forest Service
870 Emerald Bay Road, Suite 1
South Lake Tahoe, CA 96150
(530) 573-2600
Visitor Center: (530) 573-2674
www.r5.fs.fed.us/ltbmu

Malakoff Diggins State Historic Park
23579 North Bloomfield-
Graniteville Road
Nevada City, CA 95959
(530) 265-2740
http://parks.ca.gov/north/goldrush/
mdshp.htm

Mono Lake Committee
Information Center & Bookstore
U.S. 395 at Third Street
P.O. Box 29
Lee Vining, CA 93541
(760) 647-6595
www.monolake.org

National Forests Of California
www.fs.fed.us/recreation/states/
ca.shtml

National Park Reservation System
(800) 365-2267

Placer County
Public Works Dept.
(530) 889-4000
www.placer.ca.gov

Plumas National Forest
159 Lawrence St.
P.O. Box 11500
Quincy, CA 95971-6025
(530) 283-2050
www.r5.fs.fed.us/plumas

Feather River Ranger District
875 Mitchell Avenue
Oroville, CA 95965
(530) 534-6500

Sequoia National Forest
Supervisor's Office
900 West Grand Avenue
Porterville, CA 93257
(559) 784-1500
www.r5.fs.fed.us/sequoia

Cannell Meadow Ranger District
P.O. Box 6
Kernville, CA 93238
(760) 376-3781

Giant Sequoia National Monument
Contact the Sequoia Nat'l Forest
Supervisor's Office

Greenhorn Ranger District
4875 Ponderosa Drive
P.O. Box 3810
Lake Isabella, CA 93240
(760) 379-5646

Hume Lake Ranger District
35860 E. Kings Canyon Road
Dunlap, CA 93621
(559) 338-2251

Visitor Information Center
3801 Pegasus Drive (BLM Building)
Bakersfield, CA 93308
(661) 391-6088

Sierra National Forest
1600 Tollhouse Road
Clovis, CA 93612
(559) 297-0706
www.r5.fs.fed.us/sierra

**Pine Ridge-Kings River
Ranger Districts**
P.O. Box 559
Prather, CA 93651
(559) 855-5360

Stanislaus National Forest
19777 Greenley Road
Sonora, CA 95370
(209) 532-3671
www.r5.fs.fed.us/stanislaus

Calaveras Ranger District
P.O. Box 500
Hathaway Pines, CA 95233
(209) 795-1381

Tahoe National Forest
631 Coyote St.
Nevada City, CA 95959
(530) 265-4531
www.r5.fs.fed.us/tahoe/tnf

Nevada City Ranger District
631 Coyote St.
Nevada City, CA 95959
(530) 265-4531

Downieville Ranger District
15924 Highway 49
Camptonville, CA 95922
(530) 288-3656

Sierraville Ranger District
Hwy. 89 North
P.O. Box 95
Sierraville, CA 96126
(530) 994-3401
www.r5.fs.fed.us/tahoe/svrd

Tahoe National Forest (cont.)
Big Bend Visitor Center
I-80 at Big Bend-Rainbow Rd.
exit
P.O. Box 830
Soda Springs, CA 95728-0830
(530) 426-3609

Foresthill Ranger District
22830 Foresthill Road
Foresthill, CA 95631
(530) 367-2224

Truckee Ranger District
10342 Hwy. 89 North
Truckee, CA 96161
(530) 587-3558

Tulare County
Transportation Branch
(559) 733-6291
www.co.tulare.ca.us

References

Browning, Peter. 1991. *Place Names of the Sierra Nevada*. Wilderness Press.

Heizer, R.F. & Whipple, M. A. 1971. *The California Indians; A Source Book*. University of California Press.

Hill, Mary. 1975. *Geology of the Sierra Nevada*. University of California Press.

Hill, Russell B. 1986. *California Mountain Ranges*. Falcon Press.

Holliday, J.S. 1981. *The World Rushed In; The California Gold Rush Experience*. Simon and Schuster.

Hutchinson, W. H. 1969. *California: Two Centuries of Man, Land & Growth in the Golden State*. American West Publishing Company.

Irwin, Sue. 1991. *California's Eastern Sierra; A Visitor's Guide*. Cachuma Press.

McPhee, John. 1993. *Assembling California*. Farrar, Straus and Giroux.

Mitchell, Roger. 1976. *Western Sierra Jeep Trails*. La Siesta Press.

Mitchell, Roger. 1991. *Inyo Mono Jeep Trails*. La Siesta Press.

Mitchell, Roger. 1992. *Eastern Sierra Jeep Trails*. La Siesta Press.

Nadeau, Remi. 1992. *Ghost Towns & Mining Camps of California; A History & Guide*. Crest Publishers.

Olmsted, Gerald W. 1991. *The Best of the Sierra Nevada*. Crown Publishers, Inc.

Schoenherr, Allan A. 1992. *A Natural History of California*. University of California Press.

Index

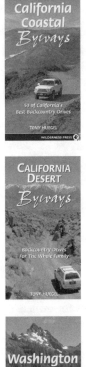

About the author

Tony Huegel is the author of six family-oriented guides for owners of sport-utility vehicles: *California Desert Byways, Sierra Nevada Byways, California Coastal Byways, Utah Byways, Colorado Byways* and *Idaho Byways*. He grew up in the San Francisco Bay Area, and is now an Idaho-based journalist.

Notes